PRAYERTIME
CYCLE C

Faith-Sharing Reflections
on the Sunday Gospels

Robert Heyer, Editor

Jean Marie Hiesberger

Mary Lou Verla

Monica Verploegen Vandergrift

James McGinnis

Mary Birmingham

Rev. Joseph Donders

PRAYERTIME
CYCLE C

*Faith-Sharing Reflections
on the Sunday Gospels*

**RENEW International
Plainfield, New Jersey**

NIHIL OBSTAT
Reverend Lawrence E. Frizzell, D.Phil.
Censor Librorum

IMPRIMATUR
Most Reverend Theodore E. McCarrick, D.D.
Archbishop of Newark

IMPRIMATUR
Most Reverend John J. Myers, J.C.D., D.D.
Archbishop of Newark
(Presentation of the Lord, Nativity of John the Baptist, Transfiguration,
Assumption, Triumph of the Cross, All Saints, All the Faithful Departed,
Dedication of St. John Lateran, Nativity of the Lord)

Cover design by James F. Brisson
Photograph © Katherine Andrews

Library of Congress Catalog Card Number: 2012916788

Main entry under title
PRAYERTIME, Cycle C
cm.
ISBN 978-1-935532-99-6
1. Church year meditations. 2. Prayer groups-Catholic Church. 3. Catholic
Church Custom and practices. 4. Common lectionary-Meditations. I.
Heyer, Robert J.,
editor, 1933- .

Published by RENEW International
1232 George Street
Plainfield, NJ 07062-1717
website: www.renewintl.org
Phone: 908-769-5400

Printed and bound in the United States of America

CONTENTS

Acknowledgments   vii

Foreword   ix

Introduction   1

Advent Season
    First Sunday of Advent   11
    Second Sunday of Advent   15
    Third Sunday of Advent   19
    Fourth Sunday of Advent   23
      Jean Marie Hiesberger

Christmas Season
    The Holy Family   29
    Second Sunday after Christmas   33
    The Epiphany of the Lord   37
    The Baptism of the Lord   42
      Jean Marie Hiesberger

Lenten Season
    First Sunday of Lent   49
    Second Sunday of Lent   53
    Third Sunday of Lent   57
    Fourth Sunday of Lent   61
    Fifth Sunday of Lent   65
    Palm Sunday of the Lord's Passion   69
      Monica Verploegen Vandergrift

Easter Season
    Easter Sunday   75
    Second Sunday of Easter   79
    Third Sunday of Easter   83
    Fourth Sunday of Easter   87
    Fifth Sunday of Easter   91
    Sixth Sunday of Easter   95
    The Ascension of the Lord   99
      Rev. Joseph Donders
    Seventh Sunday of Easter   102
    Pentecost Sunday   106
      Mary Lou Verla

Solemnities
    The Most Holy Trinity   110
    The Most Holy Body and Blood of Christ   114
      Mary Lou Verla

Season of the Year (Ordinary Time)

Second Sunday in Ordinary Time 121
Third Sunday in Ordinary Time 125
Fourth Sunday in Ordinary Time 129
Fifth Sunday in Ordinary Time 133
Monica Verploegen Vandergrift
Sixth Sunday in Ordinary Time 137
Seventh Sunday in Ordinary Time 141
Eighth Sunday in Ordinary Time 146
Ninth Sunday in Ordinary Time 150
Tenth Sunday in Ordinary Time 154
Eleventh Sunday in Ordinary Time 159
Twelfth Sunday in Ordinary Time 163
Thirteenth Sunday in Ordinary Time 167
Fourteenth Sunday in Ordinary Time 172
Fifteenth Sunday in Ordinary Time 176
James McGinnis
Sixteenth Sunday in Ordinary Time 181
Seventeenth Sunday in Ordinary Time 185
Eighteenth Sunday in Ordinary Time 189
Nineteenth Sunday in Ordinary Time 193
Twentieth Sunday in Ordinary Time 197
Twenty-First Sunday in Ordinary Time 201
Twenty-Second Sunday in Ordinary Time 205
Twenty-Third Sunday in Ordinary Time 209
Twenty-Fourth Sunday in Ordinary Time 213
Twenty-Fifth Sunday in Ordinary Time 217
Mary Birmingham
Twenty-Sixth Sunday in Ordinary Time 221
Twenty-Seventh Sunday in Ordinary Time 225
Twenty-Eighth Sunday in Ordinary Time 229
Twenty-Ninth Sunday in Ordinary Time 233
Thirtieth Sunday in Ordinary Time 237
Thirty-First Sunday in Ordinary Time 241
Thirty-Second Sunday in Ordinary Time 245
Thirty-Third Sunday in Ordinary Time 249
Last Sunday in Ordinary Time: Christ the King 253
Rev. Joseph Donders

Appendix
Solemnities and Feasts and the Sunday Celebration 257

Music Resources 313

Liturgical Calendar: Year C 321

Other Resources 324

ACKNOWLEDGEMENTS

P*RAYER*T*IME, Cycle C,* is a communal work. I wish to acknowledge and thank the following people for their creative contributions:

- Msgr. Tom Kleissler, who nourished this idea from the beginning and who invited me to be editor of this project

- Mary C. McGuinness, O.P., for her support and affirmation as well as for managing all the details of testing and publication

Authors

- Mary Birmingham, Director of Music, Liturgy, and Christian Initiation at Our Savior's Parish in Cocoa Beach, Florida

- Joseph G. Donders, Professor of Mission and Cross-Cultural Studies at Washington Theological Union

- Jean Marie Hiesberger, religious educator, author, creator, and editor of *ParishWorks* and *FaithWorks*

- James McGinnis, founder of the Institute for Peace and Justice, retreat director, and workshop leader

- Monica Verploegen Vandergrift, Director of Spiritual and Ministerial Development and visiting professor at Weston School of Theology

- Mary Lou Verla, staff member at the Office of Worship in Worcester Diocese and twelve-year veteran on her parish liturgical committee

RENEW International Staff Members

- Julie Jones
- Dolly Farrell (née Bandura)
- Kathleen Longo

Consultants

- Father John Russell, O.Carm.
- Father James M. Cafone, S.T.D.

Piloters

Small Christian Community members who piloted sessions and offered their valuable comments, from the following archdiocese or dioceses:

- Newark, NJ
- Baltimore, MD
- Hartford, CT
- Birmingham, AL
- Buffalo, NY
- Fresno, CA
- Lubbock, TX
- Portland, ME

Robert Heyer

FOREWORD

Imagine the quality of parish life if all meetings and gatherings were better focused on that commonality that brings us together in the first place—our love of the Triune God and the implementation of the life-giving mission of Jesus.

Too often, our meetings reflect models that have little connection with Gospel values. A finance committee, for example, must deal with more than strictly financial considerations. Seeking an enlightened understanding of the Church and guidance from the Holy Spirit will surely result in wiser discretion as to expenditures of parish funds.

The example above illustrates why we so often say, "An end of committee in the Catholic Church and a beginning of community!"

PRAYERTIME, Cycle C: Faith-Sharing Reflections on the Sunday Gospels is a treasured resource for adult faith formation. Begin all parish meetings—committees, societies, ministries—with *PRAYERTIME*. All parish ministries flourish when coming from a base of prayerful and scripturally rich community. Yes, an end to boring committee meetings and a beginning of community!

Small Christian communities will also love *PRAYERTIME*. Let all parish meetings and gatherings be enriched with *PRAYERTIME*!

Msgr. Thomas A. Kleissler
Co-Founder, President Emeritus
RENEW International

INTRODUCTION

PRAYERTIME, *Cycle C* offers a resource for faith sharing based on Scripture. Using the Sunday Gospels of Cycle C as the focus, meaningful reflections, focused faith-sharing questions, related actions for consideration, and prayers on each Sunday reading are proposed as sources for nourishment, renewal, and inspiration.

Each group using PRAYERTIME needs to have a prayer leader who is familiar with the service and process. This leader should obtain a copy of the Gospel reading for the Sunday. A master liturgical calendar for the how Cycle C falls across the calendar years can be found on pages 270-271. Also, the leader should ensure copies of any music selected for the reflection time are available to the participants. Appointing someone to lead the song might be helpful. Suggested songs are listed, but groups should feel free to choose their own songs. A list of music resources can be found on pages 261-268.

The service is designed to be flexible in the time required. Depending upon the size and purpose of the gathering, the process could take from ten or fifteen minutes to thirty or ninety minutes. If the meeting is the regular staff meeting or parish pastoral council meeting, the process would be shorter. If it is a seasonal small Christian community meeting, the process would be longer.

The leader is encouraged to be creative in preparing an appropriate setting for sharing and prayer, eliminating distractions as much as possible.

Prayer Service Outline

Welcome

At the first meeting or whenever the new participants attend, all are invited to introduce themselves and share why they came.

At other times, this time might be used for sharing the experiences that resulted from specific action decisions from the previous meeting.

Invitation to Pray

The leader brings the group together and allows a few moments for appreciating God's presence.

For every Sunday, as part of the opening prayer, there is at least one song suggestion. These are only suggestions, and groups should feel free to use other appropriate songs. Ideally the songs used should be ones that the members of the group know well enough to be able to sing, so that the song is an integral part and enhancement of the prayer of the group. There is, however, a certain value to learning new songs.

All of the songs suggested can be found in the standard hymnals or parish worship aids. A comprehensive guide to the author and/or composer, and publisher of these songs can be found on pages 313-320. Please remember that if you want to make copies of songs which are still under copyright, you need permission from the copyright holders. See pages 318-320 for copyright holder contact details.

For the opening prayer, the leader could use the alternative opening prayer from the Sunday liturgy, prepare another brief prayer, invite a participant to pray, or use the following suggested prayer:

Loving God and Father,
we ask your blessing upon our gathering.

Open our minds and hearts to hear your Word
and to act upon it.

Give us the love and compassion of Jesus
and the enlightenment of your Holy Spirit
as we seek your will.

We make our prayer through Jesus and the Holy Spirit who live in love with you. Amen.

After the song and/or prayer, the Scripture reading is proclaimed. This means it has been prepared. The leader should foresee this and select a good reader who will prepare. If necessary for understanding, the reader might give the context of the Scripture reading in a sentence or two, so that all may appreciate the meaning of this Gospel. Although the other Scripture readings of the day are also listed, the focus of each session is on that Sunday's Gospel. The additional readings are provided for the convenience of those who wish to refer to them.

After the reading, the leader invites everyone to take a few moments to savor a word or feeling or question that arises in each person as he or she listens to the reading. The leader then asks those who wish to share this aloud.

Invitation to Reflect on the Gospel

The leader asks someone to read aloud the commentary or have all read it thoughtfully to themselves. Each person then shares his or her response to Scripture. The questions may provide guides for this. The focus centers on how one experiences the action of God's Word in daily life.

Invitation to Group Sharing

After this reflection/sharing, the leader continues the group sharing by asking the first reflection question.

Each person should then share his or her response to the reflection and questions. The leader needs to bring each person gently into the sharing and not allow one person to dominate.

Invitation to Act

The leader decides the appropriate conclusion time to this sharing and moves on to talk about choosing a specific action. Each may choose an individual action or the group may want to do a common action. The primary consideration should be in determining a specific action (individual or group) that flows from the sharing. The actions listed are secondary suggestions.

When choosing individual actions, the leader will ask the members to share their decision with the group. When choosing a group action, the leader will guide the group in determining who will take responsibility for different aspects of the action.

Ministerial communities or committees may decide their tasks at hand are their responses. However, the task at hand need not be their only response. The Word always renews and challenges us.

At the beginning of the next session with this same group, the leader should begin by inviting people to share briefly how they carried out their action responses.

Invitation to Closing Prayer

The sharing draws to conclusion with prayer.

The leader or someone he or she invites is responsible for the closing prayer. Each service has a suggested closing prayer, and for some sessions, a song is suggested (usually a reprise of different verses of the opening song). However, the leader or participants may want to add or choose their own closing prayer.

Small Group Process

Small group/community sessions are a very important part of the parish's spiritual growth and development process. These small gatherings provide valuable opportunities for us, the people of God, to share our faith, to listen more closely to the Holy Spirit, and to witness that God has called us, and continues to touch and heal us as individuals, families, neighbors, and parishioners.

Understanding and respecting the ways adults learn is an essential part of small faith-sharing groups. It is important that the atmosphere be comfortable, warm, and friendly. Ambiguity and difference of opinion are to be expected. Each person is given the opportunity to express feelings and thoughts, examined in light of the rich scriptural tradition of our faith. Being accepted and listened to are essential ingredients of a good faith-sharing experience. There should be a true desire to listen to another's experience. A sense of humor is always helpful!

The leader/facilitator is the person who has responsibility for guiding the group through the faith sharing and prayers (or assigning them to one of the members) of the small group session. Leaders of the small groups must be well-trained for the task. By demonstrating charity and flexibility, a facilitator can effectively help the group to stay on the topic, gently include hesitant members, and develop a warm, accepting, open climate, as well as group cohesiveness.

Leaders do not provide preambles or prologues to questions; they do not frighten, shame, or argue with participants by word, gesture, expression, voice tone, or note taking. Participants may have questions about specific elements of our faith. Rather than trying to answer all questions, the facilitator may refer the questions to the pastor or parish staff to gain answers about our faith.

A leader listens carefully to the participants and asks questions only when necessary to keep the discussion moving or keep it on focus. The leader needs to be prepared by understanding beforehand the questions and the background provided in the text. However, the leader need never feel bound to a set of questions or text, but should be able to adapt to what is needed for the sharing as it moves along.

When two or more Christians share faith, we are assured that Christ is in our midst and that the life of God and gifts of the Spirit are at work in us (see Matthew 18:20). Through the small group/community sessions, we are in a very vital way opening ourselves to the Spirit's working in us and through us.

Faith-Sharing Principles and Guidelines

In an effort to keep your group/community consistent with its purpose, we offer the following Faith-Sharing Principles and Guidelines:

Theological Principles

- **Each person is led by God on his or her personal spiritual journey. This happens in the context of the Church.**

- **Faith sharing refers to shared reflections on the action of God in one's life experience** as related to Scripture and the Church's faith. Faith sharing is not necessarily discussion, problem solving, or Scripture study. The purpose is an encounter between a person in the concrete circumstances of one's life and the Word of God that leads to a conversion of heart.

- **Faith sharing is meant to serve our union with Christ, his Church, and with one another.** With the help of God's Spirit, we contribute vitality to the whole Church. We receive authoritative guidance from the Church's leadership. We are nurtured in the sacramental life. We are supported by a community of believers for our mission in the world.

- **The entire faith-sharing process is seen as prayer,** that is, listening to the Word of God as broken open by others' experience.

Small Group Guidelines

- **Constant attention to respect, honesty, and openness for each person will assist the group or community's growth.**

- **Each person shares on the level where he or she feels comfortable.**

- **Silence is a vital part of the total process of faith sharing.** Participants are given time to reflect before any sharing begins, and a period of comfortable silence might occur between individual sharings.

- **Persons are encouraged to wait to share a second time until others who wish to do so have contributed.**

- **The entire group is responsible for participating and faith sharing.**

- **Confidentiality is essential, allowing each person to share honestly.**

- **Reaching beyond the group in action and response is essential for the growth of individuals, the groups, and the Church.**

ADVENT SEASON

FIRST SUNDAY
OF ADVENT

Christ's Coming: Future, Present, Past

Invitation to Pray

Pause for a few moments of silence and enter more deeply into the presence of God.

Opening Song
O Come, O Come, Emmanuel

Proclaim the Gospel
Luke 21:25-28, 34-36
The Exhortation to Be Vigilant

Take a few minutes to savor a word, a phrase, a question, or a feeling that rises up in you. Reflect on this quietly or share it aloud.

The other Scripture readings of the day are
Jeremiah 33:14-16,
Psalm 25:4-5, 8-10, 14,
and 1 Thessalonians 3:12—4:2.

Invitation to Reflect on the Gospel

The message of this Gospel passage is simple: salvation is coming to the world and it is coming through the Son of Man. Pay attention, we are warned, for he comes when you least expect him. Ears opened, cast your eyes to what is going on around you so that you recognize him when he is near.

As we begin our preparation for the celebration of Christmas, these words remind us that Advent is a time for peace and quiet. This is an ironic contrast to the way the season is celebrated in our culture. The fast-forward pace and multiple expectations of Christmas preparation that we put on ourselves are fed by our culture and all those who are eager to "sell Christmas" to us! Why is Advent a time meant for peace and quiet? So that we can detect those hints or signals of God's presence in our lives; so that we can hear when God knocks on the door of our consciousness; so that we may respond "Yes" to God's call, just as Mary did when the "knock" came from the Angel Gabriel. The call may come in the guise of our suffering neighbor. God often calls us to pay attention to those whose needs we can attend. Our need to be still and listen opens in us opportunities to see, hear, and respond. Otherwise, the stranger will pass by us unnoticed; Jesus will not be born in our hearts.

Jesus has already come into our world in history and it is this Christmas story we prepare to hear in the coming weeks. The Scriptures tell us that Jesus will also come again at the end-time. But now, this very day, Jesus wants to come into the homes in which we dwell and into our very hearts and consciousness. It is our choice whether or not to let him be born here. Do we see and hear him? Be still and listen.

Invitation to Group Sharing

1. How can I structure "listening time" to hear God's call during this busy season?

2. How can Mary's openness to God's call serve as a model for me? To what insight or action might Jesus be leading me?

3. Realizing that Jesus is present in the people and places we least expect, what can I do for someone less fortunate?

4. What is the message in this reflection? In what way can we respond to it?

Invitation to Act

Determine a specific action (individual or group) that flows from your sharing. This should be your primary consideration. When choosing an individual action, determine what you will do and share it with the group. When choosing a group action, determine who will take responsibility for different aspects of the action. The following are secondary suggestions:

1. Commit to spending a certain part of each day this week in quiet reflection, asking the Son of Man to help you recognize his coming in another person this day and to know what action it calls you to take.

2. Decide what part of the pre-Christmas frenzy you will cut out this year so that your life will have the peace that will allow this Advent time to really be about preparing for Jesus' coming into your life throughout the coming year.

3. Perhaps you already have a sense of how you can reach out in response to Jesus' presence. Name what the situation is that needs your help and what you can do about it this week.

4. Display in a prominent place a statue or picture of Mary to be a reminder of her reflective waiting.

5. Suggest someone for whom you could, as a group, offer some kind of assistance this week. Is there a family struck with illness to whom you could bring dinner each night? Are there children who could benefit from your spending time together? Can your families join together on the weekend to do a helpful project?

Invitation to Closing Prayer

Give thanks to God (aloud or silently) for insights gained, for desires awakened, for directions clarified, for the gift of one another's openness and sensitivity. Conclude with the following:

Jesus, Son of Man, you honored us with your presence in this world during your life. You will honor us with your presence again at the end of this life.

You have nurtured us in Word and sacrament in the Church, which is your body. During this season when we prepare to celebrate your birth long ago, teach us that we can also celebrate your coming every day.

We believe you are truly present in the people around us, and especially in those whom you honored during your earthly life: those who are poor, forgotten, sick and imprisoned, those who are alone. We can be with you when we are with them in spirit, in prayer, in helping hands that lift up and comfort.

We humbly ask you to walk with us during this Advent. In the quiet of our hearts, allow us to discover you. Whenever and wherever we encounter you, may we honor you by whatever service we can give in return for the great gift of your coming on that first Christmas. Amen.

Closing Song
O Come, O Come, Emmanuel

SECOND SUNDAY
OF ADVENT

Forgiveness, Repentance, Reconciliation

Invitation to Pray

Pause for a few moments of silence and enter more deeply into the presence of God.

Opening Song
Jesus, Come to Us

Proclaim the Gospel
Luke 3:1-6
The Preaching of John the Baptist

Take a few minutes to savor a word, a phrase, a question, or a feeling that rises up in you. Reflect on this quietly or share it aloud.

The other Scripture readings of the day are
Baruch 5:1-9,
Psalm 126:1-6,
and Philippians 1:4-6, 8-11.

Invitation to Reflect on the Gospel

John the Baptist is the last of the prophets of the old law who announced the arrival of the new law in Christ. Jesus emphasized the enduring value of the law of Moses by drawing the principle of the two-fold law of love from Deuteronomy and Leviticus. Like Jeremiah and the other prophets, John proclaimed a covenant between God and us—a relationship with God who lifts up those who are poor, cares for those who are downtrodden, and exalts those who are oppressed.

St. Luke demands that Jesus' followers do no less. Our response to Jesus, he says, is to have a complete conversion, a turning away from a life that does not fulfill this charge, and turning toward God. In turning toward God, we will live out our baptism, that is, conversion to a life of service and concern for and with others.

Sometimes we think of conversion as turning away from serious sin. And yet, John the Baptist and Luke the Evangelist remind us to wake up even to the quiet parts of our lives that contain conscious and unconscious attitudes and behaviors that do not uphold Jesus' greatest commandment to love God and each other. Luke and John the Baptist also remind us, especially in Advent, to turn away from being satisfied and complacent with our present life, and make our every living day a prayer of praise and thanksgiving that is manifest in our attitudes and actions.

They call us to own up to our failings, to seek the forgiveness of God: a forgiveness that makes us stronger and more able to live the life God desires for us. When we try to live a "right" life as an individual and as a community,

"The winding roads shall be made straight, and
   the rough ways made smooth ..."

(Luke 3:5b-6; cf. Isaiah 40:4b).

Invitation to Group Sharing

1. In what ways do I experience the forgiveness of God? How does my forgiveness of others reflect that forgiveness?

2. Is there somewhere in my life where reconciliation is waiting to occur? What steps can I take to bring this about? What role does prayer play in this process?

3. How do I feel about the underlying message of both John the Baptist and Luke that repentance means offering care for those who are in need?

4. What are some concrete ways this message calls our parish community to act?

Invitation to Act

Determine a specific action (individual or group) that flows from your sharing. This should be your primary consideration. When choosing an individual action, determine what you will do and share it with the group. When choosing a group action, determine who will take responsibility for different aspects of the action. The following are secondary suggestions:

1. Alone, or with a spiritual director or a friend, take time this week to examine possible places in your life where conversion is most needed.

2. Set aside prayer time this week specifically to ask God for forgiveness. If possible, participate in the sacrament of reconciliation.

3. Determine where reconciliation is needed in your parish and how you can facilitate bringing that about.

4. Decide on a specific action to lift up those who are poor or care for those we have neglected.

Invitation to Closing Prayer

Give thanks to God (aloud or silently) for insights gained, for desires awakened, for directions clarified, for the gift of one another's openness and sensitivity. Conclude with the following:

Leader   O loving God, you promised to send your Son Jesus.

All   **Make ready the way of the Lord!**

Leader   You forgive us our failings each day.

All   **Make ready the way of the Lord!**

Leader   You came as the least among us.

All   **Make ready the way of the Lord!**

Leader   You ask us to forgive others as you
             forgive us.

All   **Make ready the way of the Lord!**

Leader   With your support we will care for those
             we have neglected.

All   **Make ready the way of the Lord!**

Leader   Be with us on our journey this Advent.

All   **Make ready the way of the Lord!**

All   **O God, our Father,
             as your prophet John the Baptist
                 instructs us,
             we ask not only your forgiveness but your
                 loving help
             that we may turn away
             from being satisfied and complacent with
                 our present lives,
             and make our every living day
             a prayer of praise and thanksgiving to you
             by our attitudes and by our actions.**

            **We ask this through your Son Jesus Christ,
             in union with the Holy Spirit.**

            Amen.

THIRD SUNDAY
OF ADVENT

Christian Morality—
"Baptized in the Holy Spirit"

Invitation to Pray

Pause for a few moments of silence and enter more deeply into the presence of God.

Opening Song

On Jordan's Bank

Proclaim the Gospel

Luke 3:10-18
The Preaching of John the Baptist

Take a few minutes to savor a word, a phrase, a question, or a feeling that rises up in you. Reflect on this quietly or share it aloud.

The other Scripture readings of the day are

Zephaniah 3:14-18a,
Isaiah 12:2-6,
and Philippians 4:4-7.

Invitation to Reflect on the Gospel

John the Baptist is trying to get his followers to pay attention: pay attention to their lives and pay attention to the coming of the Holy One. John himself only baptizes with water, but the one coming soon will actually baptize in the Holy Spirit! "Take it seriously," he wants to say. But what many of John's followers wanted to take seriously was that he was the Messiah.

John continues to tell them that nothing he does or says points to himself.

This is good advice for us, too. Like the Baptist, the good works we may do should not be done to point to ourselves. Like the Baptist, we are not the one from whom good things come.

We are trying to carry and live out the message that a life of faith and good deeds is what our baptism in the Spirit is about.

How do we live that out? The otherwise stern John the Baptist answers that it does not necessarily require that we make a momentous change in our lifestyle. Keep doing what you do, he tells the soldiers, the citizens, and the tax collectors, but be more generous with your extra coat and food; be just in all your actions. We, too, are expected to remain in our neighborhood, our state in life, our work. However, as we let the message of the Baptist pierce our consciousness, there will be simple, but perhaps radical, demands made upon our attitudes, our spirit, the quality of our work, the way we treat others around us, and those in need.

Invitation to Group Sharing

1. What various roles do I play in my life? How do I serve others in each of these roles? In what ways can I improve?

2. What can I do to ensure that, even after Advent, I will remember this message of John the Baptist: "Whoever has two cloaks should share with the person who has none. And whoever has food should do likewise" (v. 11).

3. What might John the Baptist say to our parish if we asked him, "And we, what should we do?"

Invitation to Act

Determine a specific action (individual or group) that flows from your sharing. This should be your primary consideration. When choosing an individual action, determine what you will do and share it with the group. When choosing a group action, determine who will take responsibility for different aspects of the action. The following are secondary suggestions:

1. Each day this week, focus on one role in your life and pray about how you can serve others better within that role.

2. If you have children, choose a time this week to talk about this simple but profound message of John the Baptist. Help each other name his or her "roles" and brainstorm together simple ways to be of service to others.

3. Go through your closets, and take new or clean clothes in good condition to an agency that distributes them to those in need. Continue throughout the week in daily prayer for those who will soon wear these gifts.

4. Fast one day this week in solidarity with those who have no food this day. If this is not an option due to health, try an evening fast, abstain from meat, remove snacks from your diet for a week, etc.

Invitation to Closing Prayer

Give thanks to God (aloud or silently) for insights gained, for desires awakened, for directions clarified, for the gift of one another's openness and sensitivity. Conclude with the following:

Father of our Lord Jesus Christ,
we rejoice that you sent your Son to us in Bethlehem,
and as we wait for his return at the end of time,
we live in hope.

May our hearts be filled with the joy you promised.

As caring followers of Jesus,
help us to live this week
with the message of John the Baptist
in our minds and hearts.

Help us to bring a sign of your love to those in our
lives, not that they may praise us,
but that they, too, may taste the joy
of the One who is to come in glory.

We ask these things through Jesus and the Holy Spirit.
Amen.

Closing Song
On Jordan's Bank

Fourth Sunday
of Advent

*"Blessed is she who believed that
there would be fulfillment of what
was spoken to her by the Lord."*

Invitation to Pray

*Pause for a few moments of silence and enter more
deeply into the presence of God.*

Opening Song
Hail Mary: Gentle Woman

Proclaim the Gospel

Luke 1:39-45
Mary Visits Elizabeth

*Take a few minutes to savor a word, a phrase, a
question, or a feeling that rises up in you. Reflect on
this quietly or share it aloud.*

The other Scripture readings of the day are

Micah 5:1-4a,
Psalm 80:2-3, 15-16, 18-19,
and Hebrews 10:5-10.

Invitation to Reflect on the Gospel

God is present to each of us in a variety of ways. In this
Gospel passage, Elizabeth is aware of the presence of
God in Mary. Like Elizabeth, we, too, are challenged to
become aware of the presence of God in our own lives.
How is God present to us in each person with whom we
live and work? Where is God present to us in nature; in
the stillness we allow ourselves in private prayer; in

our community worship and gatherings; in the person next to us on the bus or train or plane? This is for us to ponder and to discover even in the bustle of a fast-paced life.

Elizabeth shows us that when we see goodness, we should acknowledge it, both to the other person and to God. Such gratitude expressed creates more goodness and naming it gives us an appreciative and joyful heart. Our tiny prayer of thanksgiving joins the universe's praise to the God who comes to us each day and in many ways.

Elizabeth extols the faith of Mary, a faith not just in the words of the angel, but in the way Mary saw herself and her Child totally within the will of God. Mary surrendered to God's will freely. Today we live out God's will in a time and place much different from Mary's and Elizabeth's. But in its essence it is also quite the same as theirs. Our life, too, is to be a prayer of praise and gratitude living out God's will. We discover God's will for ourselves as did Mary, in prayer and reflection. Then, like Elizabeth, we live it out as a prayer of praise and gratitude.

Invitation to Group Sharing

1. What advice, from my own experience, would I give someone trying to discern God's will for himself or herself?

2. When I look over the past year of my life, for what or for whom am I particularly grateful ?

3. How can I celebrate and express my gratitude to others and to God in the coming weeks?

4. As we reflect on the story of God—Emmanuel—with us throughout the Scriptures, what do we as a people especially have to be grateful to God for? How can we express and celebrate this together?

Invitation to Act

Determine a specific action (individual or group) that flows from your sharing. This should be your primary consideration. When choosing an individual action, determine what you will do and share it with the group. When choosing a group action, determine who will take responsibility for different aspects of the action. The following are secondary suggestions:

1. Spend time this week writing a list of the people and gifts in your life for which you are grateful to God. Post it on the refrigerator or put it in your pocket and say a silent prayer of gratitude every time you see it.

2. Spend time alone in prayer asking for help in discovering God's will for yourself. Then, write a "mission statement" of your own life telling why you think/feel you were put on this earth and how you are and will be living that out. Reflect seriously on how this personal statement fits into your work, your hobbies, your family life, involvement in the parish, etc.

3. Seek people regularly who live with grateful hearts rather than with cynicism. Spend time with them.

4. Tell each group member how he or she has helped make God present in your time together.

Invitation to Closing Prayer

Give thanks to God (aloud or silently) for insights gained, for desires awakened, for directions clarified, for the gift of one another's openness and sensitivity. Conclude with the following:

The RENEW Prayer to Mary

Mary, you are a woman
  wrapped in silence
and yet the Word born of your yes
continues to bring life to all creation.
Mary, help us to say yes—
to be bearers of good news
  to a world waiting.

Mary, you are a virgin and a mother
empowered by the Holy Spirit.
Help us to open ourselves
to that same life-bringing Spirit.
Mary, help us to say our yes.

Mary, you are a gift of Jesus to us,
  Mother of the Church.
Look upon our world and our lives.
Pray for us to your Son
  that we might be renewed
that we might help renew
  the face of the earth.

Mary, help us to say yes. Amen.

Closing Song
Verse 3 and refrain of Here I Am, Lord

CHRISTMAS SEASON

THE HOLY FAMILY

Family Life

Invitation to Pray

Pause for a few moments of silence and enter more deeply into the presence of God.

Opening Song
> Where Charity and Love Prevail
> *or*
> Sing of Mary, Meek and Lowly

Proclaim the Gospel
> *Luke 2:41-52*
> The Boy Jesus in the Temple

Take a few minutes to savor a word, a phrase, a question, or a feeling that rises up in you. Reflect on this quietly or share it aloud.

The other Scripture readings of the day are

> *1 Samuel 1:20-22, 24-28,*
> *Psalm 84:2-3, 5-6, 9-10,*
> *and 1 John 3:1-2, 21-24.*

Invitation to Reflect on the Gospel

Jesus was found in the temple, answering the questions of the temple instructors, even putting questions to them, and replying to his mother with words that she and Joseph did not grasp. Luke related this encounter to the prophecy of Simeon that Mary would suffer in her experience of motherhood. Then the Gospel links this event, at Passover time and on the third day, to the sacrificial death of Jesus. Jesus' questions challenged

Mary to grow in faith by grappling with them as they returned to Nazareth, and their intimacy deepened. In reflecting on this incident, the virtues of forgiveness and patience are stressed. We all hurt others, sometimes deliberately out of anger or spite; most of the time out of ignorance or impetuosity. We need to give others a second chance. Later, Jesus would say we should forgive even seventy-seven times (see Matthew 18:22).

Forgiveness and patience are perhaps the most needed virtues within a family. Living side by side, day after day, we find much to forgive in each other. We all need patience to bear differences in personality, preferences, or habits. In this story of the Holy Family, we can find the same needs. Mary and Joseph displayed patience and forgiveness with the young Jesus as they sought and found him in the temple and tried to understand why he stayed behind. They are examples of how to live with forgiveness and patience.

It would seem that in practicing these ordinary family virtues of patience and forgiveness, we are doing much more than overlooking the faults of others and giving them a second chance. We are being introduced to a wonder hidden within them and within all of us together. As we, like Mary and Joseph, keep all these things in our heart and reflect upon wonders we cannot grasp, our spouses and children, our neighbors and friends are introducing us to God's presence in our midst. Together, we grow in wisdom and age and grace before God and our family, neighbors, and co-workers.

Invitation to Group Sharing

1. Which relationships in my family are most difficult? Which are most comfortable? Why?

2. What can I learn from the children, young adults, peers, and older members in my family? How do each of them speak to me a message of faith when I truly listen to him or her and reflect?

3. When has someone forgiven me or given me a second chance? How did that experience affect me?

4. What steps will I take to practice forgiveness and/or patience with a family member?

Invitation to Act

Determine a specific action (individual or group) that flows from your sharing. This should be your primary consideration. When choosing an individual action, determine what you will do and share it with the group. When choosing a group action, determine who will take responsibility for different aspects of the action. The following are secondary suggestions:

1. Spend extra time this week with your family. Strengthen your relationships by sharing activities together.

2. Reach out to someone who has no family, or no family nearby, at the present time. Perhaps invite him or her to share a meal with your family.

3. Pray for the virtue of patience in all your relationships, especially those at home. Practice patience with one person or throughout one experience this week.

4. Ask forgiveness of someone with whom you have been impatient in the past.

Invitation to Closing Prayer

Give thanks to God (aloud or silently) for insights gained, for desires awakened, for directions clarified,

*for the gift of one another's openness and sensitivity.
Conclude with the following:*

Heavenly Father,
we ask you to keep us from taking
the ordinary so much for granted.
Help us be patient with each other.

Help us appreciate all people and
see anew the mystery of godliness within them.
Give us the humility to ask for
the forgiveness we need and
the generosity to offer our own forgiveness
to others in return.
We ask this through your Son,
Jesus Christ, in union with the
Holy Spirit. Amen.

Second Sunday after Christmas

Incarnation

Invitation to Pray

Pause for a few moments of silence and enter more deeply into the presence of God.

Opening Song
Silent Night, Holy Night

Proclaim the Gospel

John 1:1-18
"And the Word became flesh ..."

Take a few minutes to savor a word, a phrase, a question, or a feeling that rises up in you. Reflect on this quietly or share it aloud.

The other Scripture readings of the day are

Sirach 24:1-2, 8-12,
Psalm 147:12-15, 19-20,
and Ephesians 1:3-6, 15-18.

Invitation to Reflect on the Gospel

This feast and this Gospel reading celebrate the Incarnation, that is, Jesus becoming human. The eternal Word of God became flesh in Jesus Christ. From that moment on, there was no denying that God's love is near to us and that God's love for us is tremendous. In sending his only Son, God gave us the opportunity to become children of God and brothers and sisters of Christ. What did we do to merit this great love? Nothing. Nothing we could ever do would merit it, but we can respond to this great gift of love. Love responds to love in likeness. Our response to this great love is to try to live our lives as Jesus taught us to live: we are to be Christians and children of God ourselves.

What is still lacking in our life that Jesus wants for us? What do we need to do to become closer to that model? As we begin a new year, we have an opportunity to reflect on that question with more clarity. We have the opportunity to resolve to put those insights into action in our daily lives.

"And the Word became flesh and made his dwelling among us ..." (v. 14). It is now our turn to make God present in the world. We have been given everything we need to do that.

Invitation to Group Sharing

1. Share specific ways in which you can more faithfully be the presence of God to your family.

2. Who is an example of someone that lives a life of care and love?

3. What can I, or we, do to start the new year with more resolve to live a life of love in response to the love God showed by the Incarnation?

Invitation to Act

Determine a specific action (individual or group) that flows from your sharing. This should be your primary consideration. When choosing an individual action, determine what you will do and share it with the group. When choosing a group action, determine who will take responsibility for different aspects of the action. The following are secondary suggestions:

1. Choose someone who seems to be struggling with his or her relationship with God and decide how to help that person feel Jesus is present to him or her also. Decide on a specific kindness you can offer.

2. Jesus came especially for the forgotten. In your prayers this week, remember those who are lonely, poor, or suffering in your community. As individuals or as a group, determine ways to respond to their needs.

3. Choose a particular project for the coming year that you will support as a sign of your gratitude for the Incarnation. Decide how you will give it your time, regular financial support, or the benefit of your talents.

4. In the coming week, participate in the celebration of Mass daily (or visit a church on your lunch break or on your way to or from work, grocery shopping, etc.) as an expression of your gratitude to God for sending Jesus into our world.

Invitation to Closing Prayer

Give thanks to God (aloud or silently) for insights gained, for desires awakened, for directions clarified, for the gift of one another's openness and sensitivity. Conclude with the following:

Pray Psalm 98, alternating in two groups:

I.   Sing a new song to the LORD,
　　　who has done marvelous deeds,
　　whose right hand and holy arm
　　　have won the victory.

II.   The LORD has made his victory known;
　　　has revealed his triumph for the nations
　　　　to see,

    I.   has remembered faithful love
           toward the house of Israel.
       All the ends of the earth have seen
           the victory of our God.

    II. Shout with joy to the LORD, all the earth;
           break into song; sing praise.

    I.   Sing praise to the LORD with the harp,
           with the harp and melodious song.

    II. With trumpets and the sound of the horn
           shout with joy to the King, the LORD.

    I.   Let the sea and what fills it resound,
           the world and those who dwell there.

    II. Let the rivers clap their hands,
           the mountains shout with them for joy,

    I.   Before the LORD who comes,
           who comes to govern the earth,
       to govern the world with justice
           and the peoples with fairness.

All **Be with us, Jesus,**
      as we go about our lives this week.

      Watch over our days and nights.

      Help us be aware
      that the lives we lead each day
      are our response
      to the great love shown to us
      in your coming into this world.

      We pray in the name of the Father,
      you, the Son,
      and the Holy Spirit.

      Amen.

THE EPIPHANY
OF THE LORD

Epiphany

Invitation to Pray

Pause for a few moments of silence and enter more deeply into the presence of God.

Opening Song
We Three Kings

Proclaim the Gospel

Matthew 2:1-12
The Visit of the Magi

Take a few minutes to savor a word, a phrase, a question, or a feeling that rises up in you. Reflect on this quietly or share it aloud.

The other Scripture readings of the day are

Isaiah 60:1-6,
Psalm 72:1-2, 7-8, 10-13,
and Ephesians 3:2-3a, 5-6.

Invitation to Reflect on the Gospel

The feast of the Magi is an event of great symbolism. The Epiphany commemorates the Savior coming not only to the Jewish people but to all peoples: Gentile, pagan, "outsiders" of all kinds. God's love leaves no one untouched. The Magi, wise in the ways of stars, discovered Jesus. God reveals himself to them in signs. Each of us has "stars" or signs in our own life which, if followed, lead us also to God. Like the Magi, our search must be guided by the Word of God in the Scriptures.

Signs come in all forms: it may be the love we receive from another person; the good example of someone who tries to live by the Gospel; an insight that comes in our prayer and reflection; observing someone who is not self-centered; the challenge from a friend to look beyond our own little world; the cry of a child; something we read in the newspaper that calls out to us; even sickness or tragedy in our lives. It is up to us to pay attention and read the signs around us. They will lead us to God if we look with openness and with eyes of faith. When we make a response to those signs, we may not find a baby in a manger, but we will find the face of God in those whom we reach (or those who reach us).

This feast is also a feast of unity. Jesus came to all and we are all one under God's love. Where is there unity in our own world? Where is there disunity? Every family, every parish community, every nation sees the results of the evil of intolerance. As we reach out to those looked down upon, or those considered "outsiders," we do our part to bring about the unity that God envisioned in sending his Son, Jesus, to us.

Invitation to Group Sharing

1. The Epiphany is about Jesus coming for all people. In what ways might I, or we, forget that truth and treat some people or groups as "outsiders"?

2. Have I ever been treated as an "outsider"? How did I feel?

3. What are ways I, or we, can reach out to those who might feel excluded? What will we do?

Invitation to Act

Determine a specific action (individual or group) that flows from your sharing. This should be your primary consideration. When choosing an individual action, determine what you will do and share it with the group. When choosing a group action, determine who will take responsibility for different aspects of the action. The following are secondary suggestions:

1. Make time each day this week to reflect on who or what are signs calling you to take an action that will lead you to God.

2. Reach out to someone who is looked down upon or excluded and help him or her feel included. Have a cup of coffee or a meal together. Consider inviting him or her to join a group to which you belong.

3. Take time in your group or within a relevant parish committee to brainstorm who are the "outsiders" in your parish or neighborhood. Plan some specific action to change that situation.

Invitation to Closing Prayer

Give thanks to God (aloud or silently) for insights gained, for desires awakened, for directions clarified, for the gift of one another's openness and sensitivity. Conclude with the following:

Pray Psalm 72, alternating in two groups:

I.   O God, give your judgment to the king;
        your justice to the son of kings;
      That he may govern your people with justice,
        your oppressed with right judgment,

II.   That the mountains may yield their bounty
        for the people,
      and the hills great abundance,

I.   That he may defend the oppressed among

the people,
save the poor and crush the oppressor.

II. May he live as long as the sun endures,
like the moon, through all generations.

I. May he be like rain coming down upon
the fields,
like showers watering the earth,

II. that abundance may flourish in his days,
great bounty, till the moon be no more.

I. May he rule from sea to sea,
from the river to the ends of the earth.

II. May his foes kneel before him,
his enemies lick the dust.

I. May the kings of Tarshish and the islands
bring tribute,
the kings of Arabia and Seba offer gifts.

II. May all kings bow before him,
all nations serve him.

I. For he rescues the poor when they cry out,
the oppressed who have no one to help.

II. He shows pity to the needy and the poor
and saves the lives of the poor.

I. From extortion and violence he frees them,
for precious is their blood in his sight.

II. Long may he live, receiving gold from Arabia,
prayed for without cease, blessed day
by day.

I. May wheat abound in the land,
flourish even on the mountain heights.
May his fruit increase like Lebanon's,
his wheat like the grasses of the land.

II.   May his name be blessed forever;
      as long as the sun, may his name endure.
  May the tribes of the earth give blessings
      with his name;
      may all the nations regard him as favored.

I.   Blessed be the LORD, the God of Israel,
      who alone does wonderful deeds.

II.   Blessed be his glorious name forever;
      may all the earth be filled with the
      LORD'S glory.

All   **Amen and amen.**

THE BAPTISM
OF THE LORD

Mission of Jesus; Mission of Each Christian

Invitation to Pray

Pause for a few moments of silence and enter more deeply into the presence of God.

Song

Joy to the World

Proclaim the Gospel

Luke 3:15-16, 21-22
The Preaching of John the Baptist

Take a few minutes to savor a word, a phrase, a question, or a feeling that rises up in you. Reflect on this quietly or share it aloud.

The other Scripture readings of the day are

*Isaiah 40:1-5, 9-11,
Psalm 104:1b-4, 24-25, 27-30,
and Titus 2:11-14; 3:4-7.*

Invitation to Reflect on the Gospel

The baptism of Jesus is a dramatic moment in his life and is also an important symbolic moment for us. We who have received baptism are told that we, too, are God's beloved; we, too, are freed from sin; we, too, are filled with the Holy Spirit and chosen to live out the same mission as Jesus. The baptism described here is a window to our own destiny, our own call to live in Christ. Jesus' baptism revealed that God loved him and had chosen him. Our baptism reveals that we are especially loved and chosen by God and belong to his Body, the Church.

Jesus' mission was now to go into the world and preach that God's love is for all people. Ours is the same: to go into the world in which we live and preach the love of God. Our world is our family; our neighborhood and friends; our co-workers and parishioners; the people all around the world with whom we can be connected through the news, the Internet, and the organizations that reach across our continents.

How do we preach? We preach by our words and our actions, just as Jesus did. But we evangelize in our own way. We do this first through prayer that supports a loving attitude toward those around us, and by being truly present and attentive to the people in our immediate life. We also evangelize by using our talents to help others, our voice to speak up for those who are voiceless, our financial contributions to help those who are in need, the power of the pen and ballot box to help bring justice into the world, and our time to volunteer to be of service in the many places working to lift up those who are downtrodden in our world. When we put flesh to the works of mercy, we, too, are truly the sons and daughters on whom God's favor rests.

Invitation to Group Sharing

1. Who or what are some contemporary examples of the mission of Jesus being lived by individuals, institutions, and organizations in our own age? How do these speak to me?

2. What does my baptism mean to me?

3. In what ways have I been called to witness the love of God?

4. How can we continue the mission of Jesus, especially to those who are in need?

Invitation to Act

Determine a specific action (individual or group) that flows from your sharing. This should be your primary consideration. When choosing an individual action, determine what you will do and share it with the group. When choosing a group action, determine who will take responsibility for different aspects of the action. The following are secondary suggestions:

1. Pray over the many opportunities you have to continue Jesus' mission and your own baptismal call. Choose one action you will concentrate on in the coming weeks. Share that decision with another person and ask him or her to pray for your perseverance.

2. Challenge yourself to a kind of outreach that you have resisted in the past. Ask someone to partner with you to give you support in doing it.

3. Choose a project in your own area and volunteer as a group to work on it. Come back together in a month to talk about it.

4. Send a monthly contribution to someone or an organization continuing the work of Jesus in a way or place you cannot; for example, Maryknoll Fathers & Brothers, P.O. Box 304, Maryknoll, NY 10545-0304 or RENEW International, 1232 George Street, Plainfield, NJ 07062-1717, www.renewintl.org.

Invitation to Closing Prayer

Give thanks to God (aloud or silently) for insights gained, for desires awakened, for directions clarified, for the gift of one another's openness and sensitivity. Conclude with the following:

Leader	Jesus, you were born into our world as one of us.
Response	**We praise and thank you, O God.**
Leader	Jesus, you came to bring God's love.
Response	**We praise and thank you, O God.**
Leader	Jesus, you taught us how to live.
Response	**We praise and thank you, O God.**
Leader	Jesus, we want to live out your mission.
Response	**We praise and thank you, O God.**
Leader	Jesus, we know you are with us still and nourish us in Word and sacrament.
Response	**We praise and thank you, O God.**
All	**Be with us, O loving Savior, as we continue the works you did during your time on earth.**
	Each of us has a limited time to carry out your mission.
	Help us to use each day of this life to make a better life for others that we may all share in the joy and peace you came to bring.
	We pray in the name of the Father, you, the Son, and the Holy Spirit. Amen.

LENTEN SEASON

First Sunday of Lent

Conversion and Lenten Renewal

Invitation to Pray

Pause for a few moments of silence and enter more deeply into the presence of God.

Opening Song

Lord, Who throughout These Forty Days
or
Led by the Spirit

Proclaim the Gospel

Luke 4:1-13
The Temptation in the Desert

Take a few minutes to savor a word, a phrase, a question, or a feeling that rises up in you. Reflect on this quietly or share it aloud.

The other Scripture readings of the day are

Deuteronomy 26:4-10,
Psalm 91:1-2, 10-15,
and Romans 10:8-13.

Invitation to Reflect on the Gospel

Jesus has fled to the desert to sort through a powerful experience of affirmation by his Father. In a profoundly public moment of baptismal surrender, he is confirmed as the "Son of God." He must grapple in all humility with the ramifications of this identity. His own understanding of himself would lead to a profound self-surrender to his Father's will.

In the desert, the devil plays on all the conventional meanings associated with the image of "the Son of God": miracle worker, political hero, leader. While Jesus' life will testify to many of these, Jesus knows intuitively that there is more to this identity than the tradition indicates. In his hunger for clarity and truth, Jesus questions these limited cultural assumptions about the Messiah. In response to each challenge, Jesus drew upon God's Word in the Book of Deuteronomy.

Digging down into his recent experience of the Father, Jesus moves past physical desires and needs, past glory and fame, past seeking validation and pressing for proof. He moves beyond his own hungers and ambitions, as well as the expectations of others, to the essence of this intimate relationship of "Sonship" with the Father. He must live "Sonship" within the boundaries of human flesh and time, and prevent ambition from jeopardizing God's timing. The Father's message indicated that being Son entailed service. This means moving slowly while listening to the Spirit who will direct him, to stand with those who suffer, and be an advocate for those made marginal in society.

Jesus' self-understanding in relationship to the Father undergoes a process of self-emptying love. Each Lent, we enter into a conversion process, seeking clarity in our own faith journey. Moving more deeply into intimacy with God challenges our cultural and personal assumptions about what it is to become more fully Christian. Conversion of heart requires us to move beyond ambition and cultural assumptions to listen to God who heals, forgives, and stands humbly with those who are needy.

Invitation to Group Sharing

1. There are many things in society that tempt us. Name three against which I must struggle.

2. To what specific act of spiritual growth am I being called this Lent?

3. When in my own life have I reached out to those on the margins for the sake of Christ? What is the first step I, or we, can make toward standing as advocates for people on the margins of society?

4. How can I, or we as a group, be stretched to be compassionate leaders?

Invitation to Act

Determine a specific action (individual or group) that flows from your sharing. This should be your primary consideration. When choosing an individual action, determine what you will do and share it with the group. When choosing a group action, determine who will take responsibility for different aspects of the action. The following are secondary suggestions:

1. Determine a Lenten resolution that will lead you to live more deeply with God, for example, spend 15 minutes each day in reading the Scriptures or in quiet prayer.

2. For a Lenten project, encourage each group member to select an individual who lacks support and concern, and reach out personally to that person throughout the season.

3. To raise your consciousness, between today and the next meeting, prayerfully listen for persons who may be overlooked by the parish or society and at your next meeting strategize ways to address their neglect, for example, persons with disabilities, those

who are elderly, homebound, prisoners, or those condemned to die.

4. Fast one day this week in solidarity with those who go hungry or for peace and nonviolence. Be specific regarding conflict, that is, those orphaned by war, or school violence victims. Cut articles from magazines or newspapers and incorporate pictures and faces of those in your daily prayer. Fast after noon or abstain from meat, if fasting all day is not an option due to health.

Invitation to Closing Prayer

Give thanks to God (aloud or silently) for insights gained, for desires awakened, for directions clarified, for the gift of one another's openness and sensitivity.

Conclude with the following:

Beloved God and Father,
as Jesus chose
to respond gently to the Spirit
and patiently stand with those
who were in need,
give us the same courage
to step outside
the social conventions of our lives
and reach out
to those we have forgotten or neglected.

We pray this,
knowing that you want all good
for us and for those we serve,
in Jesus' name. Amen.

SECOND SUNDAY
OF LENT

Faith and Spiritual Journey

Invitation to Pray

Pause for a few moments of silence and enter more deeply into the presence of God.

Song

Do Not Fear to Hope
or
Out of Darkness

Proclaim the Gospel

Luke 9:28b-36
The Transfiguration

Take a few minutes to savor a word, a phrase, a question, or a feeling that rises up in you. Reflect on this quietly or share it aloud.

The other Scripture readings of the day are

Genesis 15:5-12, 17-18,
Psalm 27:1, 7-9, 13-14,
and Philippians 3:17—4:1.

Invitation to Reflect on the Gospel

Jesus is about to face the most trying period of his life in this world: his conviction as a criminal, the walk to Calvary, and his subsequent execution. The events leading up to his crucifixion may have been as painful emotionally as the dying itself—betrayal, misunderstanding, abuse, and desolation. The seeming absence of God the Father in the most crucial hour of his life must have been excruciating for one so intimately united to the divine. These experiences deepened Jesus' faithfulness and his perseverance in the journey of the Spirit. He invited the apostles into this profound moment of revelation.

The Transfiguration is an incredible blessing, filling Jesus with the support, grace, and inspiration he needed to walk those difficult final days. Jesus is affirmed by the great figures of his tradition, who represent the law and the prophets. Even though he will be rejected by the representatives in his day of religious and civil law and the prophetic tradition, he is held up by the wisdom figures of ancient times. This illumination will have to carry him through the dark days of confusion, insecurity, and terror that will begin as soon as he comes down the mountain.

Each of us needs touchstones or special memories to return to when we face the crosses in our journey. These "God-moments" may be more subtle than a transfiguration on a mountaintop, but their impact can help sustain us if we recognize them. These touchstone events may be recalled when we reflect on the ways in which we have been inspired at other times of trial. Personal "transfigurations" may reveal themselves when we begin to share our story of struggle and faith. What has sustained us in trial can continue to do so if we allow ourselves to savor them later on! God's revelation continues in each re-visitation of gratitude and marvel.

Invitation to Group Sharing

1. The celebration of Eucharist recalls many of the great events of our faith tradition—the passion, death, and resurrection of Christ. In what ways does

participation in Mass help me to be inspired and sustained?

2. Where are the special memories or "aha" moments that have sustained me in the past and even now sustain me? Looking back on these memories or moments, how have I seen the Spirit working in my life?

3. During Lent, how can I, or we, be a light to others in their time of betrayal, misunderstanding, and desolation?

Invitation to Act

Determine a specific action (individual or group) that flows from your sharing. This should be your primary consideration. When choosing an individual action, determine what you will do and share it with the group. When choosing a group action, determine who will take responsibility for different aspects of the action. The following are secondary suggestions:

1. At Mass, reflect prayerfully on the beautiful words of the eucharistic prayer.

2. Make your prayer time after Communion a period of gratitude for the transfiguration moments in your life.

3. Establish an outreach effort to people housed in institutions who may feel lonely and afraid. Ask them to tell you their stories of survival in hard times. Listen to them. Be with them. Affirm their stories.

4. Choose to support in a personal way a person who has suffered a misunderstanding or a betrayal.

Invitation to Closing Prayer

Give thanks to God (aloud or silently) for insights gained, for desires awakened, for directions clarified, for the gift of one another's openness and sensitivity.

Conclude with the following:

Jesus, you have the mind of the prophets
and the heart of the law.

We stand in wonder
at this transfiguration event,
marveling at God's generous support of you
as you walked toward your death.

Open our eyes to see
how we can be attentive to
your revelation in our struggles
and in the stories of others.

Allow us to clasp hands with you in support
and reach out to others in times of trial.

We pray this,
knowing that you desire justice
and mercy for all of us. Amen.

THIRD SUNDAY
OF LENT

Social Justice and the Social Dimension of Sin

Invitation to Pray

Pause for a few moments of silence and enter more deeply into the presence of God.

Song

Isaiah 58

Proclaim the Gospel

Luke 13:1-9
The Fig Tree

Take a few minutes to savor a word, a phrase, a question, or a feeling that rises up in you. Reflect on this quietly or share it aloud.

The other Scripture readings of the day are

Exodus 3:1-8a, 13-15,
Psalm 103:1-4, 6-8, 11,
and 1 Corinthians 10:1-6, 10-12.

Invitation to Reflect on the Gospel

Today's reading calls us to task. As in the case of the impatient owner of a vineyard who has allowed a barren fig tree to remain in a privileged place in his garden, despite its unfruitfulness, God's patience with our complacency wears thin. We presume great generosity and forgiveness of God with regard to our weakness and ignorance, but, in turn, what should God be able to presume from us? Does God's generosity of heart require something from us?

Perhaps the most challenging aspect of this parable is the demand placed upon us that we repent and bring about change. Our fruitfulness must be displayed, first of all, in repentance that reflects a personal commitment to turn our faces toward God. God's desire for us is a personal engagement in relationship with God, but the fruitfulness does not remain strictly on the personal level. This change of heart must display itself in the ways we live out our daily lives. How does a renewed relationship with God manifest itself in our relationships with family and those closest to us? Will it be reflected in a new awareness of our Christian call to work for a more just society?

It is easy to lapse into a complacent routine in our Christian lives. We depend on God's compassion with regard to our limitations. Inferred from the parable of the fig tree is a responsibility to change, to do what is necessary so that not only we, but our world, will be bettered. Christ takes our part and pleads for more time, while he tends to our hearts and ministers to our ignorance. In time, we will be called to account for our gifts and the contributions we made toward making the world a better place, one that is more humane and just.

During Lent, let us look to see if we have a tendency to settle for the status quo, and challenge ourselves with God's aid to see where our fruitfulness needs to be encouraged.

Invitation to Group Sharing

1. When I look honestly at my own life right now, where do I see complacency creeping in?
2. Where do I feel discomfort with this challenge from Scripture? Why do I feel this way?

3. What local problems most disturb me? What would be a first step toward addressing one of these problems locally?

Invitation to Act

Determine a specific action (individual or group) that flows from your sharing. This should be your primary consideration. When choosing an individual action, determine what you will do and share it with the group. When choosing a group action, determine who will take responsibility for different aspects of the action. The following are secondary suggestions:

1. Spend some time in prayer asking God to help you overcome complacency. Then choose an action to make your immediate world or the larger world a better place.

2. Reach out to renew a relationship with a family member, neighbor, or friend you may have neglected.

3. Invite a social worker or police officer to visit your group during Lent to inform you of the hidden injustices within your community. Afterward, decide how you can help overcome some injustice.

Invitation to Closing Prayer

Give thanks to God (aloud or silently) for insights gained, for desires awakened, for directions clarified, for the gift of one another's openness and sensitivity.

Conclude with the following:

Lord Jesus Christ,
it is hard for us
to hear your challenge to our complacency.

You call us to repent
and share your good news with others.

And yet we often overlook
these responsibilities in our world.

Help us shake off our lethargy
and bravely begin again this Lent
to look at the challenge the world puts before us.

Help us to *act* consciously
in union with you
to make this world a healthier and safer place
for all who may be afraid or in danger.

We pray this
knowing you desire
the fullness of life for all. Amen.

FOURTH SUNDAY OF LENT

Dignity of the Individual Person

Invitation to Pray

Pause for a few moments of silence and enter more deeply into the presence of God.

Song

Hosea

Proclaim the Gospel

Luke 15:1-3, 11-32
The Prodigal Son

Take a few minutes to savor a word, a phrase, a question, or a feeling that rises up in you. Reflect on this quietly or share it aloud.

The other Scripture readings of the day are

Joshua 5:9a, 10-12,
Psalm 34:2-7,
and 2 Corinthians 5:17-21.

Invitation to Reflect on the Gospel

"Come home. Please … just come home. Forget the transgressions and the mistakes you have made along the way. Let them go. Don't let them separate us anymore. I want you home." What parent, who deeply loves his or her child, would not echo this sentiment of the prodigal father, who heartily welcomes the return of his wayward son? Jealousy and resentment lock up the older son, who has generously given so much to his father in daily fidelity. But the father sees the errant young man and simply goes to the heart of the issue: welcome home!

We resonate with different characters of this story throughout our lives. In youth, we may understand the gambling young man who experiments with life and risks it all. Later on, after years of toil and sweat, we may identify more with the older son, critical of the behavior of others. Finally, in our elder years, we may stand in the shoes of a seasoned parent, who puts aside obstacles and merely wants loved ones close. God asks us to love always, regardless of circumstance.

Our experience of God may go through similar transitions. Our images of God can become transformed gradually in our human encounters throughout life. Gradually, we discover the generosity of God, the hospitality of One who yearns for us to come home. This can affect the way we treat ourselves, too. Slowly, if we let it, the experience will bring us gradually to forgive ourselves of shortsightedness in our choices, of resistance to reconciliation, and of distance from God. What is important changes. We want to rest in the arms of our Father. This is what matters. All we desire is to be at home with God.

Invitation to Group Sharing

1. At this time in my life, with whom in the story do I most identify? Why?

2. What does "welcome" feel like? Tell a story of feeling "welcomed."

3. Are there persons I know who are estranged from me, in need of reconciliation and welcome? How will I welcome them and be reconciled?

Invitation to Act

Determine a specific action (individual or group) that flows from your sharing. This should be your primary consideration. When choosing an individual action, determine what you will do and share it with the group. When choosing a group action, determine who will take responsibility for different aspects of the action. The following are secondary suggestions:

1. Write, call, or visit someone with whom you need to be reconciled.

2. Plan a Reconciliation Service with a special outreach to alienated Catholics.

3. Bring families together for discussion on how to begin the healing process with members who are estranged from each other. Possibilities include inviting a guest speaker or holding a dinner before or after a Reconciliation Prayer Service.

4. Identify other religious groups in which there may exist historical tensions with your parish. Construct a plan for dialogue and reconnection with those groups.

5. Develop a relationship with programs that reach out to alienated youth, for instance, Covenant House, and begin financial and emotional support that brings the lost home.

Invitation to Closing Prayer

Give thanks to God (aloud or silently) for insights gained, for desires awakened, for directions clarified, for the gift of one another's openness and sensitivity.

Conclude with the following:

Loving Father,
you are patient with our wanderings,
understanding of our lapses in fidelity,
and desirous of our return.

Lead us back, Beloved,
to the home which is in your heart,
to the place of self-acceptance,
tolerance, and forgiveness.

Give us what we need
to reach out to those
who are alienated
in confusion, pain, or misunderstanding.

Teach us how to be as welcoming of others
as we are always welcomed by you.

We pray this,
trusting in your magnificent love for us,
in Jesus' name
and through the power of the Holy Spirit. Amen.

FIFTH SUNDAY OF LENT

Outreach to the Alienated

Invitation to Pray

Pause for a few moments of silence and enter more deeply into the presence of God.

Song
Loving and Forgiving

Proclaim the Gospel

John 8:1-11
The Woman Caught in Adultery

Take a few minutes to savor a word, a phrase, a question, or a feeling that rises up in you. Reflect on this quietly or share it aloud.

The other Scripture readings of the day are

Isaiah 43:16-21,
Psalm 126:1-6,
and Philippians 3:8-14.

Invitation to Reflect on the Gospel

A woman accused of adultery is dragged before Jesus. She is not condemned for prostitution or promiscuity, but the relational sin of adultery, a violation against marriage and social stability. We know little of her story, nor is Jesus told anything of the circumstances surrounding her transgression. He asks for no explanation. Rather, he notes her humiliation, surrounded by self-righteous men who disregard their own sinfulness.

Jesus is handed the heavy burden of judgment. He is caught between the law which is meant to protect the sanctity of marriage and the vulnerability of the woman who stands before him. He knows the intention of entrapment by those who drag her there. It seems an impossible situation.

First let us recall a story from the Desert Fathers in which Abba Moses is called to an assembly to judge a guilty brother. Initially, he refuses to go, but is prevailed upon. So, he fills a leaky old basket with sand and walks to the assembly.

"Father, what is this?" the brothers inquire as he arrives.

"My sins are running behind me and I do not see them. So how can I come today to judge the sins of another person?"

The brothers relent and forgive their brother. Jesus chose mercy as his solution to judgment. Abba Moses deferred to humility and refused judgment. Our sins are all around us. Others see what we do not. The challenge is to remain mindful of our own vulnerabilities and, thus, arrest our tendencies to reduce another. We are to judge actions, not persons, as good or evil. Through thoughtful awareness of our own inclination to sin, we discover that we share the same humanness of the ones we judge. If we cultivate compassion and forgiveness toward ourselves, are we not less likely to pick up that stone and throw it?

Invitation to Group Sharing

1. Has an event in my own life changed my attitude of righteousness? (For example, one husband shared the story of his tendency to judge the divorced, until his wife left him.)

2. Considering my tendency to judge, when do I get hooked into throwing stones?

3. Are there persons within our community who have been isolated through judgment?

4. What means of reconciliation can we inaugurate for a person or group alienated from the parish?

Invitation to Act

Determine a specific action (individual or group) that flows from your sharing. This should be your primary consideration. When choosing an individual action, determine what you will do and share it with the group. When choosing a group action, determine who will take responsibility for different aspects of the action. The following are secondary suggestions:

1. Work to establish a relationship of respect with someone you have judged harshly.

2. If your parish does not already have a group for Divorced and Separated Catholics, initiate one as a healing process for people alienated in this way.

3. As a group, volunteer at a soup kitchen to feed those whose lives have become more vulnerable than your own and remind yourselves of our common humanity. Consider starting a soup kitchen if one does not already exist.

Invitation to Closing Prayer

Give thanks to God (aloud or silently) for insights gained, for desires awakened, for directions clarified, for the gift of one another's openness and sensitivity.

Conclude with the following:

Benevolent God and Father,
you love us as a parent loves a wayward child.

We ask your forgiveness of our tendency
to judge our brothers and sisters.

We stand humbly before you,
begging for your grace and insight.

Help us to become mindful
of the areas where we
forget our humility
and reduce another through
judgment and self-righteousness.

Give us the freedom through your Spirit
to embrace the sinful other
as we acknowledge
our own vulnerability and blindness.

We praise your generosity and graciousness, Lord,
and surrender to your wisdom and mercy,
through Jesus Christ, our Lord. Amen.

Palm Sunday
of the Lord's Passion

Letting Go of Power and Control;
the Value of Suffering

Invitation to Pray

Pause for a few moments of silence and enter more deeply into the presence of God.

Song

Listen to a recording of Andrew Lloyd Webber's *Pie Jesu*

Proclaim the Gospel

Luke 22:14—23:56 or Luke 23:1-49
The Sentence of Death

Take a few minutes to savor a word, a phrase, a question, or a feeling that rises up in you. Reflect on this quietly or share it aloud.

The other Scripture readings of the day are

Isaiah 50:4-7,
Psalm 22:8-9, 17-20, 23-24,
and Philippians 2:6-11.

Invitation to Reflect on the Gospel

This week we are going to hear many words describing the traumatic suffering and dying of the One whom we call "Lord." It may be too much for us to comprehend. It proved too much for the disciples to take in, also. If we really move into the event, the climax of Jesus' life overwhelms us. Suffering is overwhelming for us. It is jolting to meet something so phenomenal around which we cannot maneuver. We experience helplessness. Somehow, though, we must dwell within it, stand in awe of it, and pray through it.

In times of suffering, we return to an awareness of our own human frailty. It is a place of humility, recognizing God as Creator and ourselves as finite creatures within the larger reality. We, like the disciples, experience our limits. We are not in ultimate control. That is God's domain. So, too, is the reason for suffering and the miracle of Resurrection in God's domain.

Holy Week is a week of suffering. The passion of Our Lord is suffering that connects him with us in our humanity in a very definitive way. Suffering may be a meeting place between God and ourselves. In suffering we grow in solidarity with Christ and with those he loves. His suffering is an icon of our own suffering, a window of opportunity that points us to our Creator. God, who is infinite, reaches out in staggering humility to touch us in that pain. God, who took on human flesh, dies at the hands of those whom he came to enlighten. Accepting the humiliation, the betrayal, and the smallness of human minds, Jesus lives out his last days at the mercy of the merciless.

During Holy Week, our hearts meld with Christ in his passion and we walk humbly with all who presently suffer. We breathe with them in the knowledge that we are one in this human existence, honoring this common bond in wonder, empathy, and respect. As we recall this most precious event within the Christian tradition, we are called to enter more deeply into the reality of pain and persecution in our world. We also know the profound promise of a light that will not be overcome by deep shadows. Again, at this time in history, let us promise to live in that light so that sin and injustice will be overcome.

Invitation to Group Sharing

1. Where have we as individuals or as a group witnessed suffering this past year?

2. When do I suffer or feel helpless in my own life? What gift can it bring to me? Can I see God touching or meeting me in this suffering?

3. During Holy Week, how can I walk more intentionally with people who are suffering? What will I do?

Invitation to Act

Determine a specific action (individual or group) that flows from your sharing. This should be your primary consideration. When choosing an individual action, determine what you will do and share it with the group. When choosing a group action, determine who will take responsibility for different aspects of the action. The following are secondary suggestions:

1. Determine a specific amount of time you will spend in quiet reflection, journeying with the Lord in his suffering.

2. Make a point to visit someone who has been enduring a lengthy illness. Continue throughout the week to pray for their awareness of the Lord's presence.

3. Prepare and display in your parish a contemporary Stations of the Cross with photographs from your area, depicting people who are experiencing Calvary. Invite others to join you in this effort.

4. Determine how you will share Resurrection joy with those who are unemployed or homeless, those who are refugees or distanced from family, and/or those who suffer isolation due to illness, age, or sexual orientation.

5. Plan a parish outreach day of Resurrection joy.

Invitation to Closing Prayer

Give thanks to God (aloud or silently) for insights gained, for desires awakened, for directions clarified, for the gift of one another's openness and sensitivity.

Conclude with the following:

God our Father, you know our suffering
and our resurrections.

You walk with us in times
of despair and misunderstanding
as you walked with Jesus
to his betrayal and crucifixion.

So many people in our world
suffer the pain of persecution and alienation.

During this sacred week,
we ask that you open our hearts
to those nearby who are suffering,
even as we raise our eyes to Jesus on the cross.

Give us the courage to step out
and help them carry their burden
in whatever way we can.

Let us not overlook our chance
to be in solidarity with you
and ease your load through our care for them.

We pray this in Jesus' name. Amen.

EASTER SEASON

EASTER SUNDAY

Jesus Is Risen

Invitation to Pray

Pause for a few moments of silence and enter more deeply into the presence of God.

Song
Ye Sons and Daughters

Proclaim the Gospel
John 20:1-9
The Empty Tomb

Take a few minutes to savor a word, a phrase, a question, or a feeling that rises up in you. Reflect on this quietly or share it aloud.

The other Scripture readings of the day are
Acts of the Apostles 10:34a, 37-43,
Psalm 118:1-2, 16-17, 22-23,
and Colossians 3:1-4 or 1 Corinthians 5:6b-8.

Invitation to Reflect on the Gospel

Today's Gospel account of the Resurrection ends abruptly in mid-story. We hear of shock, puzzlement, and awe; there is no rejoicing. When the three arrived in the garden, they saw the unexpected. "For they did not yet understand the scripture, that [Jesus] had to rise from the dead" (v. 9). Mary Magdalene, Peter and "the other disciple whom Jesus loved" (v. 2) have not seen Jesus, only the empty tomb.

Mary approached Jesus' tomb in the last dark hours preceding the dawn. Seeing that the stone was moved away, she must have been alarmed. Jesus had spoken of being raised from the dead, but it was such an incomprehensible thing—even after witnessing the raising of Lazarus. In the Gospel account, we hear that Peter entered the tomb and registered the details of what he saw—the wrappings were in two different places; the body was not there. We are told that when the beloved disciple entered the tomb "he saw and believed" (v. 8). Even though they did not wholly comprehend what they experienced, each of them took a different step in the movement toward faith: fear, confusion, and acceptance.

In our lives we are often faced with situations and experiences that stretch our ability to see and believe. Often, that stretching comes during times of distress or upheaval … loss or change of job or home, a new baby's arrival, an older child's departure, etc. Changes can often be doorways to resurrection, even as we grope around in the insecurity of the change.

As believers, we have been nurtured and fed by the stories and accounts of our forbearers in faith. Mary Magdalene ran breathless in the dark, Peter surveyed the situation, and the beloved disciple remembered what Jesus had said. Living life amidst the unknown and the insecurity of change requires faith in the promise of the Resurrection, even when all we see is an empty tomb.

Of this faith, hope is born. From out of this faith and hope, a radical joy can erupt and we can then proclaim, "YES! Jesus is risen! It is as he said it would be!"

Invitation to Group Sharing

1. Does my life sufficiently reflect the happiness and joy of living out my faith in the Resurrection of Jesus?

2. Is there someone I know who lives in a way that truly bears witness to the power of the Resurrection? Share who that person is and how they bear witness.

3. When have I been stretched to "see and believe" through challenging circumstances?

4. How can we be people of Resurrection to others who are experiencing uncertainties or transitions in their own lives?

Invitation to Act

Determine a specific action (individual or group) that flows from your sharing. This should be your primary consideration. When choosing an individual action, determine what you will do and share it with the group. When choosing a group action, determine who will take responsibility for different aspects of the action. The following are secondary suggestions:

1. Take time this week to become better acquainted with the image of the empty tomb. Read each of the Gospel accounts about the tomb and Jesus' Resurrection.

2. Resolve in a particular way to bring joy into the life of another person this week. Be open to receive new life from another this week.

3. Think about members of your family and friends with small children: do any of them need a break? If so, offer to help.

4. Contact an organization in your community that is a homeless shelter, a Habitat for Humanity project, a job-search center, a place that serves people in

transition or people who may be standing in an "empty tomb." See if there is some concrete way you or your group can help.

Invitation to Closing Prayer

Give thanks to God (aloud or silently) for the gift of Jesus' Resurrection this day. Conclude with the following:

Faithful God,
During this Easter season
we stand in astonishment at the empty tomb.

Your mercy and power,
evident in raising Jesus to life
are more than we can comprehend.

Help us to receive with humility
the grace you offer to us
through Jesus' Resurrection and new life.

Direct us in the ways
we may, in turn, share this abundant grace
with all those around us.

With full hearts, and in Jesus' name,
we offer you praise and thanksgiving
for the amazing love you pour out on us. Amen.

SECOND SUNDAY OF EASTER

Doubting to Professing

Invitation to Pray

Pause for a few moments of silence and enter more deeply into the presence of God.

Opening Song
> We Have Been Told
> *or* We Walk by Faith

Proclaim the Gospel
> *John 20:19-31*
> Appearance to the Disciples

Take a few minutes to savor a word, a phrase, a question, or a feeling that rises up in you. Reflect on this quietly or share it aloud.

The other Scripture readings of the day are

> *Acts of the Apostles 5:12-16,*
> *Psalm 118:2-4, 13-15, 22-24,*
> *and Revelation 1:9-11a, 12-13, 17-19.*

Invitation to Reflect on the Gospel

This Gospel tells us of the first two appearances Jesus made to his gathered disciples after his Resurrection. Both times he appears through locked doors; both times he greets them with the phrase, "Peace be with you" (v. 21a). Jesus is quick to provide assurance and comfort to the ones who followed him and served with him in his earthly life. They are living in fear because their association with Jesus has put them at odds with the powerful. They begin to grasp that what God is doing through Jesus utterly changes the reality of what their life will be from this point on.

The commissioning that happens next is nearly as astonishing as the Resurrection itself. With his words, Jesus brings those very human people into his own relationship with God: "As the Father has sent me, so I send you" (v. 21b). They are to carry on with his work. He does not speak to them about healing the sick and raising the dead; he speaks to them of forgiveness and gives them his own authority over sin! He offers an invitation to explore in a startling new way, the image of God within themselves ... that image which is compassion and forgiveness.

Then there is Thomas. Jesus gently chides and challenges Thomas for his need to "see for himself," but he does not humiliate Thomas. Even in his doubting, Thomas is treated with compassion, forgiveness, and respect. Thomas then goes on to proclaim most profoundly his own profession of faith, "My Lord and my God!" (v. 28). And in this movement from doubt to faith, Thomas stands as proxy for us. His doubts and questions echo our own. God knows the human heart. The signs that Jesus performed are recorded, and we are given the story of Thomas' encounter with Jesus so "that you may [come to] believe that Jesus is the Messiah, the Son of God, and that through this belief you may have life in his name" (v. 31).

Invitation to Group Sharing

1. What are my "locked doors" of fear that Jesus wishes to pass through and bring comfort and assurance?

2. Jesus says to us, "Peace be with you." In what ways do I find that peace reflected, or not sufficiently reflected, in my life?

3. When I doubt, what helps me regain the balance of faith?

4. In what ways can I or we offer comfort, forgiveness, and freedom to those of our community who suffer from doubt?

Invitation to Act

Determine a specific action (individual or group) that flows from your sharing. This should be your primary consideration. When choosing an individual action, determine what you will do and share it with the group. When choosing a group action, determine who will take responsibility for different aspects of the action. The following are secondary suggestions:

1. Chronicle your own faith story: your first experiences of Jesus progressing from fear to comfort to commissioning; doubting to professing. Keep it simple; focus on specific experiences and responses. Share it with another.

2. Make an effort to be aware of someone around you who may need to hear the story of your faith journey. Do not be afraid to identify with Thomas!

3. Host a night of sharing faith stories in your home or your parish. Invite others to listen attentively and be aware of any connection to their own faith stories.

4. Thomas spoke of the need to see Jesus' wounds in order to believe in his resurrected life. If there is none already, consider forming a group for those who are bereaved and may be in need of seeing concrete proof of Jesus' life and presence.

Invitation to Closing Prayer

Give thanks to God (aloud or silently) for insights gained, for desires awakened, for directions clarified, for the gift of one another's openness and sensitivity. Conclude with the following:

Gracious God and Father,
the human heart is often slow to grasp
the impact of the Resurrection on all creation,
and on our own lives as well.

When we doubt, you give us the comfort of your peace.

Strengthen us for the challenge
and the blessing of bearing your image.

Fill us with compassion and forgiveness,
so that we reflect your image more clearly.

Help us to be signs of Jesus' resurrected life
in our homes, our parish, and our community.

With full hearts, and in Jesus' name,
we offer you praise and thanksgiving
for the amazing love you pour out on us. Amen.

THIRD SUNDAY
OF EASTER

Come and Eat

Invitation to Pray

*Pause for a few moments of silence and enter more
deeply into the presence of God.*

Opening Song
Lord, You Have Come
or
In the Breaking of the Bread

Proclaim the Gospel
John 21:1-14
Appearance to the Seven Disciples

*Take a few minutes to savor a word, a phrase, a
question, or a feeling that rises up in you. Reflect on
this quietly or share it aloud.*

The other Scripture readings of the day are

*Acts of the Apostles 5:27-32, 40b-41,
Psalm 30:2, 4-6, 11-13,
and Revelation 5:11-14.*

Invitation to Reflect on the Gospel

Jesus' followers have begun to resume their usual
routines: Peter, Thomas, Nathanael, Zebedee's sons,
and two unnamed disciples are at the Sea of Tiberias
and head out to go fishing. Jesus has appeared to them
previously, yet when he calls to them from the shore,
after an unsuccessful night of fishing, they do not
recognize him at first. Only after they had cast their

nets on the opposite side of the boat, as he had instructed them, did they know it was he. An explosion of joy erupts as Peter jumps into the water and swims toward Jesus!

Jesus greets them with a fully prepared breakfast at the shore. He knows they have worked hard and are tired and hungry. This meal carries an echo of the Passover celebration: a meal that reminds the people of their history with God and God's faithful presence throughout that history. It is also reminiscent of the feeding of the multitude: he knows the importance of satisfying physical hunger if people are ever to recognize their need for God. In all these appearances, Jesus is bringing his followers through the first mystagogia, a time of opening up the mysteries of his death and Resurrection in the daily living out of their lives. He shows them the reality of his Resurrection by eating in their presence.

In this Gospel, Jesus shows us how to care and minister to one another. Whether it was feeding a multitude, or just a small band of hungry people, Jesus attended to the needs of the body and spirit. We must be attentive to whatever needs may be presented. As we go about our daily lives, how will we develop this Christlike awareness?

At every turn, we are confronted with a profound hunger for hope, acceptance, forgiveness, and healing, not to mention an adequate portion of daily bread. How can we respond to these needs? Those who are hungry must hear and recognize Christ's voice. Let our invitation to come and eat resonate loudly enough, so those who are hungry may hear and recognize our voice as the voice of Christ.

Invitation to Group Sharing

1. Describe a time you were really hungry in your spiritual life … a time when you felt you were anxious for God. Then share where you found the answer to your need.

2. What are the hungers I see most clearly in my own community?

3. How does our reception of the Eucharist strengthen us to reach out and meet the needs of those who are hungry?

4. How can we be the voice of Christ, in our community and beyond, offering provision for the hungers of the spirit, as well as the hungers of the body?

Invitation to Act

Determine a specific action (individual or group) that flows from your sharing. This should be your primary consideration. When choosing an individual action, determine what you will do and share it with the group. When choosing a group action, determine who will take responsibility for different aspects of the action. The following are secondary suggestions:

1. During your next eucharistic thanksgiving, reflect on how you might help meet the physical and spiritual hunger of others. Then do it!

2. "Adopt" an elderly person who may not get out very often; invite him or her to your home for dinner and conversation, or bring a meal to his or her home and share it.

3. Become involved in a local food pantry or soup kitchen.

4. Take turns volunteering to research any legislation (local or national) that addresses the issue of hunger

in your community. Help to keep that issue in people's minds, and look for solutions.

5. Research if local restaurants and supermarkets would donate day-old food to a local food pantry or soup kitchen. Offer to deliver food, provide volunteers to package, etc.

Invitation to Closing Prayer

Give thanks to God (aloud or silently) for the daily bread that nourishes our bodies as well as our spirits. Conclude with the following:

Generous God,
thank you for the homes we have
and the food on our tables.

You alone know the hungers we bear,
and how they can best be satisfied.

As we look to you for our nourishment,
open our eyes to the hungers around us
and, with the Spirit of Jesus,
give us the voice to call out the invitation,
"Come! Eat!" Amen.

FOURTH SUNDAY OF EASTER

The Good Shepherd

Invitation to Pray

Pause for a few moments of silence and enter more deeply into the presence of God.

Opening Song

The King of Love My Shepherd Is
or Shepherd Me, O God

Proclaim the Gospel

John 10:27-30
My Sheep Hear My Voice

Take a few minutes to savor a word, a phrase, a question, or a feeling that rises up in you. Reflect on this quietly or share it aloud.

The other Scripture readings of the day are

Acts of the Apostles 13:14, 43-52,
Psalm 100:1-3, 5,
and Revelation 7:9, 14b-17.

Invitation to Reflect on the Gospel

"Good Shepherd Sunday," as this Sunday in the liturgical year has become known, can be shadowed in sentimentality. The image of a man standing in the midst of a flock of sheep, holding his staff, gazing contentedly around is a common theme in sacred art. It is comforting, yet rather passive.

The statements that Jesus makes in this brief Gospel passage are anything but passive: "*My* sheep hear …

I know them ... *they follow* me ... *I give* them *eternal life, and they shall never* perish. *No one can* take ... *My Father, who has given them to me, is greater than all ...*" (vv. 27-29; emphasis added). This does not conjure an image of country life. In fact, in the verses just before this we see that these statements are a response Jesus gives the religious leaders when they say to him, "If you are the Messiah, tell us plainly" (John 10:24). At the same time, there is a forcefulness and an intimacy in this passage. "The Father and I are one" (v. 30). Not only does Jesus say that we are his, but the Father has given us to him and it is with the Father's hand that we are protected.

Jesus demonstrates a real possessiveness, not in a negative way, but rather in a relational way: "I am not going to let you go! In my relationship with the Father, you belong to me, to us! Therefore, *you* be possessive with those whom I have given you. *You* stay faithful, *you* forgive, *you* go after the one who has wandered off!"

Invitation to Group Sharing

1. Have I ever felt like a "wandering sheep"?

2. Have I ever been "shepherded" by Jesus? Explain.

3. When have I tried to help a "wandering sheep" come back to the Good Shepherd? What happened?

4. Many of the youth in our parishes are still developing the ability to know Jesus' voice. How might we help them with that essential part of their spiritual lives?

Invitation to Act

Determine a specific action (individual or group) that flows from your sharing. This should be your primary consideration. When choosing an individual action, determine what you will do and share it with the group. When choosing a group action, determine who will take responsibility for different aspects of the action. The following are secondary suggestions:

1. If there is a family member who seems to have wandered from your family or the faith, let us try to spend time with that person. Try to contact them if they are not close by. Do this especially at a time when he or she is hurting or in need. Share your story of how faith has had meaning in your life. Pray especially for him or her this week.

2. As a parish, pray publicly and regularly for the youth in your community.

3. Reach out to someone recently widowed or someone in need.

4. Invite your Christian youth group to lead an event at your parish; for example, hold an activities fair or pot luck supper and promote positive ways to know Jesus. This may be done in collaboration with neighboring CYOs or with the help of the diocesan youth ministry.

Invitation to Closing Prayer

Give thanks to God (aloud or silently) for his protective care, the promise of eternal life and for the "flock" with whom we share his love. Conclude with the following:

Leader   "My sheep hear my voice ..." (v. 27).

All   **Lord Jesus, help us to follow you faithfully and to offer assistance to our brothers and sisters who may wander.**

Leader   "I give them eternal life ..." (v. 28).

All   **Lord Jesus,**
             teach us to know the ways
             we can begin to live and share eternal life
             while in this world.

Leader   "The Father and I are one" (v. 30).

All   **Lord Jesus,**
             thank you for sending your Holy Spirit
             to bring us into the intimacy
             of your relationship with the Father.

             Enlarge our hearts to embrace those
             who have wandered from you,
             and help us to love and protect them
             with the heart of a shepherd. Amen.

FIFTH SUNDAY
OF EASTER

Disciple of Love

Invitation to Pray

Pause for a few moments of silence and enter more deeply into the presence of God.

Opening Song

Where Charity and Love Prevail
or
Ubi Caritas

Proclaim the Gospel

John 13:31-33a, 34-35
The New Commandment

Take a few minutes to savor a word, a phrase, a question, or a feeling that rises up in you. Reflect on this quietly or share it aloud.

The other Scripture readings of the day are

Acts of the Apostles 14:21-27,
Psalm 145:8-13,
and Revelation 21:1-5a.

Invitation to Reflect on the Gospel

Jesus has made it very clear what kind of love he is passing on to his disciples: love that requires the offering of our very selves to one another, and the larger community. This selfless love is impossible without the conviction and commitment of faith as its foundation. Because his faith is built in relationship, Jesus is a model for us. He sees himself in relation to the Father, "Now is the Son of Man glorified, and God is glorified in him" (v. 31). He sees himself in relation to his followers, "My children, I will be with you only a little while longer" (v. 33). And it is all within the bond of love that moves outward: "As I have loved you, so you also should love one another" (v. 34b).

Jesus' command to "love one another" (v. 34b) often calls us to work together to accomplish a greater good. The goal of collaboration, that is, working together, calling forth, respecting, recognizing, and encouraging each other's gifts has become the topic for many workshops and training sessions. The challenges of the ordained and laity, recognizing their capabilities and responsibilities, have been nourished and renewed by the gift of the Spirit, (cf. the documents of Vatican II). Changing expectations and understanding come slowly. Yet come they will, when we dare to listen to Jesus' imperative: "Love one another" (v. 34b).

And yet, the real work begins when we turn to one another in love. We know we need God's presence to do this. Giving our hearts with the love the new commandment calls us to give is made possible with faith. Believing in God and loving each other foolishly, without reservation or judgment, make real our relationships. Only then, can it reflect back to God, bear witness to our walk with Christ, and move us out to the world, a world in desperate need of that love.

Invitation to Group Sharing

1. How does the Eucharist uniquely bring us into deep union with our Triune God and with one another?

2. Which of my relationships are centered around my relationship with God? How does that impact these relationships?

3. What movements toward collaboration do I see in my parish? In my workplace? In my family? Where can I enhance collaboration in my life?

4. Many in our community, neighborhood, or town may know that we attend a Catholic Church. What do we do to show that we are Jesus' disciples? How do we love one another, both within our community and other communities?

Invitation to Act

Determine a specific action (individual or group) that flows from your sharing. This should be your primary consideration. When choosing an individual action, determine what you will do and share it with the group. When choosing a group action, determine who will take responsibility for different aspects of the action. The following are secondary suggestions:

1. Take time to consider whether your preparation for and participation in the Eucharist sufficiently reflect the deep union to which you are called.

2. Select a person or group with whom you need to be in better collaboration. Determine how you will improve that relationship.

3. Organize an ecumenical walk-a-thon or something similar, to raise funds and commitment for a community food pantry, childcare center, or mentoring program.

4. Read the life of Blessed Mother Teresa, Dorothy Day, or someone committed to change in the area of social justice. Take some time to reflect upon how

she or he lived the commandment: "Love one another" (v. 34b).

Invitation to Closing Prayer

Give thanks to God (aloud or silently) for his love. Conclude with the following:

Lord our God,
it is your love that sustains us,
binds us to one another,
and calls us out into the world.

Stretch us to move beyond
our own limitations,
so that in all our actions
your love will be present
to bring about forgiveness, healing, and justice.

With grateful hearts,
we thank you
for your amazing love.

In Jesus' name we pray. Amen.

Sixth Sunday of Easter

Peace Is My Gift to You

Invitation to Pray

Pause for a few moments of silence and enter more deeply into the presence of God.

Opening Song

You Are All We Have

Proclaim the Gospel

John 14:23-29

The Advocate

Take a few minutes to savor a word, a phrase, a question, or a feeling that rises up in you. Reflect on this quietly or share it aloud.

The other Scripture readings of the day are

Acts of the Apostles 15:1-2, 22-29,
Psalm 67:2-3, 5-6, 8,
and Revelation 21:10-14, 22-23.

Invitation to Reflect on the Gospel

Parting words! Parting gifts! When we are about to leave a place for an extended period, what we say to those we are leaving behind takes on extra significance. Though we hear this Gospel during the Easter season, Jesus is speaking to his disciples during the Passover meal just before he is arrested and led away. He is trying to prepare them for something they cannot yet comprehend, and he offers assurances of the most profound kind. He offers them precious gifts—the

Father's love and most intimate presence; the promise of deeper understanding and continued revelation by the power of the Holy Spirit; the gift of *shalom*, his own peace, which bears no resemblance to the peace the world gives.

We, too, are the recipients of these gifts. Through our Baptism, partaking of the Eucharist, receiving forgiveness through Reconciliation, and the sealing of our lives with the Holy Spirit in Confirmation, the Church tangibly passes on the gifts that Jesus left. Though we receive these sacraments individually, we celebrate them communally. As these sacraments serve to connect us to God, they also make us into the Body of Christ, the presence of Christ in the world today.

Jesus understood that if his followers were to carry on his work, he would need to provide the tools. He said the Holy Spirit would come to instruct and remind; we have the sacraments that draw us to God together, and also call us out into the world, as Jesus was present in the world. "… My peace I give to you" (v. 27). This peace is the *shalom* of the Jewish people: when all is right with God and his creation. Understood in that way, this gift of his peace is a call to action. It is now up to us to feed the hungry, clothe the naked, proclaim liberty to captives, and to announce a year of favor from the Lord. How do we go about accomplishing this work?

Invitation to Group Sharing

1. Is there a time when I had to leave loved ones, or someone had to leave me, and I was unsure as to when I would see them again? What did I say? What was said to me?

2. How do the sacraments of Eucharist and reconciliation help me in my efforts to serve Jesus? How do they strengthen me?

3. Tell of a time when you felt the *shalom* talked about in this Scripture: when all is right with God and his creation. How did it come about?

4. Where and how can I be an agent of peace?

Invitation to Act

Determine a specific action (individual or group) that flows from your sharing. This should be your primary consideration. When choosing an individual action, determine what you will do and share it with the group. When choosing a group action, determine who will take responsibility for different aspects of the action. The following are secondary suggestions:

1. Take some time to reflect on what the sacraments mean to you. Perhaps write down these reflections in a journal, or share them with a spiritual director.

2. As much as your time allows, offer to assist with the sacramental preparation that goes on in your parish, either with children or with adult formation.

3. Determine a way to make your love more practical by directing it toward a neglected person or a local needy cause.

Invitation to Closing Prayer

Give thanks to God (aloud or silently) for the promise of assurance, the blessing of peace.

Conclude with the following:

Faithful God,
you have given us yourself
in Word and in sacrament

so that we may see you
with eyes of faith.

As we live out our days,
help us to be authentic reflections
of your presence within us.

Thank you for choosing to dwell
within and among us.

Grant us the courage and passion
to be bearers of your peace
in a turbulent world.

In Jesus' name we pray. Amen.

THE ASCENSION
OF THE LORD

Already In and Yet Out

Invitation to Pray

Pause for a few moments of silence and enter more deeply into the presence of God.

Opening Song
How Beautiful on the Mountains

Proclaim the Gospel
Luke 24:46-53
Ascension

Take a few minutes to savor a word, a phrase, a question, or a feeling that rises up in you. Reflect on this quietly or share it aloud.

The other Scripture readings of the day are

Acts of the Apostles 1:1-11,
Psalm 47:2-3, 6-9,
and Ephesians 1:17-23.

Invitation to Reflect on the Gospel

Jesus, who had been living with the apostles for three years, went that day up to heaven. He was the same Jesus who had been telling them that he felt such oneness with them. He had compared their union with him as forming one living organism, one plant, one body: he is the vine, they are the branches; he is the head, they are the body.

When that head, Jesus Christ, one with us in our humanity, entered heaven, it was made possible for us, too, to reach heaven. No wonder that Luke tells us that they went back to Jerusalem full of joy.

When you want to keep people out of your house, you may put bars in front of your windows. Those bars should be so close to each other that no one would be able to put his or her head in between, because wherever a head can pass, the body can get through, too. Anyone assisting at a birth knows that once the head of the newborn is through, the rest of the body will follow without further difficulty.

Where the head leads, there the body follows: if our head is already in heaven, then, in a sense, so are we. That is what he promised before he went. He not only promised his disciples that they would follow him, but also that he was going to prepare a place for them.

Just before he left them, Jesus told his disciples that he would clothe them with power from on high. He gave them a task, the same task he gives to us. With that power in us, we are able to realize God's realm, God's reign, here around us in our world.

Invitation to Group Sharing

1. Is there an instance in my life when "heaven touched the earth," and the power given from above was experienced?

2. How could our parish community better celebrate the Eucharist, the Body and Blood of Jesus Christ, and help to make the connection between heaven and earth?

3. In what ways can I be more joyful this week in my relationships with family, friends, and/or co-workers?

Invitation to Act

Determine a specific action (individual or group) that flows from your sharing. This should be your primary consideration. When choosing an individual action, determine what you will do and share it with the group. When choosing a group action, determine who will take responsibility for different aspects of the action. The following are secondary suggestions:

1. Be joyful in your daily dealings this week, sharing the joy of those disciples who returned to Jerusalem.

2. Reread and reflect on today's Scripture passage in your daily prayer.

3. Look around you this week to see where you might experience a "heaven on earth" experience.

Invitation to Closing Prayer

Give thanks to God (aloud or silently) for insights gained, for desires awakened, for directions clarified, for the gift of one another's openness and sensitivity. Then pray together pausing after each line:

Almighty God, Loving Father,
thank you for the gift of the body and blood
of your Son Jesus.

We ask you to make real in our daily lives
the power of the Holy Spirit
he has given to us.

Help us to be the people you call us to be,
and to fulfill the call you have given us. Amen.

SEVENTH SUNDAY
OF EASTER

That They May Be One

Invitation to Pray

Pause for a few moments of silence and enter more deeply into the presence of God.

Opening Song
Deep Within

Proclaim the Gospel
John 17:20-25
Prayer of Jesus

Take a few minutes to savor a word, a phrase, a question, or a feeling that rises up in you. Reflect on this quietly or share it aloud.

The other Scripture readings of the day are
*Acts of the Apostles 7:55-60,
Psalm 97:1-2, 6-7, 9,
and Revelation 22:12-14, 16-17, 20.*

Invitation to Reflect on the Gospel

There is almost a sense of listening to another's conversation as we hear the proclamation of this Gospel. The tenderness, intimacy, and passion we hear in Jesus' words are utterly disarming. We are given glimpses of the eternal familial nature of the relationship between Jesus and the Father.

Jesus has just finished praying for the disciples, and now he turns his thoughts toward those of us who will come to faith as a result of their word. In his prayer,

Jesus speaks passionately of his desire for believers to be united to each other, with him, and the Father in their relationship: "so that they may all be one, as you, Father, are in me and I in you" (v. 21a). The unity for which Jesus prays is not an end in itself; his desire is for the Church to be a very part of the love that exists between the Father and himself, "that the world may believe that you sent me" (v. 21b). Jesus prays that the world may recognize God's saving love in the life and action of the Church.

During these days of the Easter season, we hear stories of the beginnings of the Church. With compassion and tenderness, Jesus brings his disciples through the initial shock and confusion that followed the Resurrection. He assures them, instructs them, and helps them to see that they are *essential* to continuing the work he started. Though this Gospel, like last week's, occurs before his death and Resurrection, Jesus' prayer is not bound by time and chronology. Similarly, the unity of the Church is not bound by time and chronology. The Church today is as connected to those gathered behind locked doors, as it is to the parish across town, as it will be to the parishes of the future. The unifying force is the Church's participation in the saving love of God. How do I live in that love?

Invitation to Group Sharing

1 Is there someone I know who seems to have a natural ability for bringing people together for a common goal? What is it about her or him that makes this so?

2. How well do we (as individuals, as a group, as a parish) reflect the unity for which Jesus so passionately prayed?

3. Talk about the possibility of establishing a close relationship with a small Christian community in a different culture or nation. Contact RENEW International for further information: 908-769-5400, www.renewintl.org.

4. What can we do to reach beyond our parish and share Christ's love?

Invitation to Act

Determine a specific action (individual or group) that flows from your sharing. This should be your primary consideration. When choosing an individual action, determine what you will do and share it with the group. When choosing a group action, determine who will take responsibility for different aspects of the action. The following are secondary suggestions:

1. As you pray the Creed at Mass, take time to consider your unity with people all over the world who are praying those same words.

2. Choose a sister parish in a developing country. Put to action the saving love of God in common prayer and communication with them.

3. As a parish, make an effort to pray for nearby congregations, regardless of their tradition, in your town or neighborhood. Contact them in a letter, telling them of your prayers; invite them to do the same.

4. With the pastor's support, consider the possibility of arranging cooperative community efforts among the youth groups of some various Christian congregations.

Invitation to Closing Prayer

Give thanks to God (aloud or silently) for the love that binds all things together.

Conclude with the following:

Lord Jesus,
thank you for the invitation
to participate in the loving energy
that exists between you and the Father.

We are in awe of your generosity,
and grateful for the reality.

Help us to take to heart the unity for which you prayed.

Your Church in the world has suffered many fractures.

Grant that we may be healers and signs of your reign,
so that those who do not know you
will be drawn in by your love,
as evidenced by our actions.

We offer this prayer
through the inspiration of your Holy Spirit. Amen.

PENTECOST SUNDAY

Come, Holy Spirit

Invitation to Prayer

Pause for a few moments of silence and enter more deeply into the presence of God.

Opening Song
On Holy Ground

Proclaim the Gospel
John 14:15-16, 23b-26

Take a few minutes to savor a word, a phrase, a question, or a feeling that rises up in you. Reflect on this quietly or share it aloud.

The other Scripture readings of the day are

Acts of the Apostles 2:1-11,
Psalm 104:1, 24, 29-31, 34,
and 1 Corinthians 12:3b-7, 12-13 or Romans 8:8-17.

Invitation to Reflect on the Gospel

"I will ask the Father, and he will give you another Advocate to be with you always" (v.16). The same Spirit that separated the earth from the sky and the sea; the same breath that was breathed into Adam now comes to rest on a group of frightened people and a new Church is born. We celebrate the remarkable feast of Pentecost as the birthday of the Church. The origins of the Church now lay with common people moved by the Spirit of God to follow after Jesus of Nazareth, before they had any idea what was going to be asked of them.

Matching the awesome drama of the Gospel is the action and excitement of today's first reading from the second chapter of Acts. The upper room is filled with wind, fire, and noisy exclamations of God's marvelous deeds, reaching the ears of the passers-by in the street. The Word of God cannot be contained! The creative energy of the Holy Spirit breathes new life back into the people, establishes the Church, and anchors it within Jesus' relationship with the Father. "Whoever loves me will keep my word, and my Father will love him, and we will come to him and make our dwelling with him" (v. 23). God's saving work is to be carried on by all those left behind.

The fire and wind swirled through the Church again when Pope John XXIII called for another Pentecost, the Second Vatican Council. Calling down the power of the Holy Spirit, the Church entered an intense time of profound self-examination. The movement of the Holy Spirit compels us to reflect continually upon everything, from how we worship, to why we pray, to who we are in the world. The power of the Holy Spirit is the life of all Christians; as a Church, we are called to reach beyond our own borders and find our place within the whole body of believers. We are to offer the witness of the kingdom of God to society and the global community.

Invitation to Group Sharing

1. Spiritually speaking, when was the last time I paused to take a breath, temporarily setting aside schedules, parish commitments, and other obligations, allowing myself to connect in a new way to the Holy Spirit?

2. On a daily basis, how often am I aware of God's Holy Spirit within me? How might I more frequently call upon the power of the Holy Spirit with expectancy?

3. By loving Jesus and keeping his Word, we each become a dwelling place for him and the Father. In what specific ways can I open the doors of that dwelling place to the people with whom I interact on a daily basis?

4. In what creative ways is the Spirit moving, inviting, and challenging me? How will I respond?

Invitation to Act

Determine a specific action (individual or group) that flows from your sharing. This should be your primary consideration. When choosing an individual action, determine what you will do and share it with the group. When choosing a group action, determine who will take responsibility for different aspects of the action. The following are secondary suggestions:

1. Contact the local retreat houses in your area, or ask a friend for a recommendation, and try to schedule a retreat for yourself.

2. In your personal prayer life, try to remove yourself from any attachment to sin and open yourself to the power and direction of the Holy Spirit.

3. As a group, contact your neighboring congregations and begin to foster connections and interest in organizing an ecumenical Pentecost celebration for next year.

4. Examine the evangelizing efforts your parish makes in reaching out to the global community. Establish ties with a missionary organization that is involved with works of mercy and evangelization.

5. Invite to your parish a speaker from a missionary community. Offer an evening for reflection and prayer to the Holy Spirit. For suggestions call your diocesan office.

Invitation to Closing Prayer

Give thanks to God (aloud or silently) for the movement of the Holy Spirit in your own life, and in the life of the Church. Conclude with the following:

Most Holy Spirit,
you were present with the Father and the Son
when all of creation was called into being.

Your moving presence
took a small group of people and
made it into a new communion that is your Church.

Make us worthy of your constant presence.

Divine Advocate,
direct our actions as individuals
and as a Church,
so that all we do
will reflect to the world
the love and presence of God. Amen.

THE MOST
HOLY TRINITY

Father, Son, Spirit

Invitation to Pray

Pause for a few moments of silence and enter more deeply into the presence of God.

Opening Song
God, Beyond All Names

Proclaim the Gospel
John 16:12-15
Jesus' Departure

Take a few minutes to savor a word, a phrase, a question, or a feeling that rises up in you. Reflect on this quietly or share it aloud.

The other Scripture readings of the day are
Proverbs 8:22-31,
Psalm 8:4-9,
and Romans 5:1-5.

Invitation to Reflect on the Gospel

In celebrating the Trinity at our liturgy today, we celebrate the greatest mystery of our faith. When Jesus speaks of the Father and the Spirit, it is in relation to himself and his connection to the relationship between the Father and the Spirit: "Everything that the Father has is mine; for this reason I told you that he will take from what is mine and declare it to you" (v. 15). Three Persons, one God. Distinct identities, yet a communication so complete the "lines" often seem blurred.

In Jesus' public life, we see the centrality of his relationship with the other Divine Persons. The Father spoke of him, calling him his beloved Son, after Jesus rose from the waters of baptism. The Spirit led him into the desert just before he embarked on his ministry. But Jesus did not cling proudly to his position as Second Person of the Trinity:

"Who, though he was in the form of God,
    did not regard equality with God
        something to be grasped.

Rather, he emptied himself,
    taking the form of a slave,
    coming in human likeness …"

(Philippians 2:6-7)

In obedience to his Father, Jesus had become fully human. With the power of the Holy Spirit, he worked to bring humanity back into relationship with God.

"But when he comes, the Spirit of truth, he will guide you to all truth" (v. 13). The same Spirit that hovered over the waters, that stirred in Mary's womb, that raised Jesus from the dead, is the same Spirit of truth who will guide the Church to all truth. As members of the Church, the Body of Christ on earth, we have been invited, gathered, and commissioned to carry on the creative, redemptive, and sanctifying work of the Trinity.

Empowered by the Holy Spirit, in communion with the Father through the Son, we are embraced in the interrelatedness of the Trinity. God calls us to stand in solidarity with Jesus. This solidarity is based on prayer and obedience to God's will, on embracing all people, on prophetically speaking the truth of the Church's teaching even when it is unpopular, and on sacrificing ourselves for others. In this solidarity, we are able to hear the cries of those who are poor, be agents of reconciliation, and bring hope to those who are hopeless.

Invitation to Group Sharing

1. In what persons or in what events of my life do I clearly see God at work?

2. What relationships in my life reflect the loving relationships of the Trinity? If I am having difficulty in a relationship, what steps can I take to bring that relationship into greater harmony with myself and God?

3. How do I stand in my relationship with God's poor in their struggles? How can I be God's presence in their lives? What will I do?

Invitation to Act

Determine a specific action (individual or group) that flows from your sharing. This should be your primary consideration. When choosing an individual action, determine what you will do and share it with the group. When choosing a group action, determine who will take responsibility for different aspects of the action. The following are secondary suggestions:

1. As Catholics, we often make the Sign of the Cross with very little thought. Take some time to think about what it means to bless ourselves and others with that simple, yet powerful, Trinitarian gesture. Be mindful in your prayers this week of your gleaned insights.

2. Pay some special attention to the important relationships in your life that may be neglected due

to busyness or over-commitment. Determine one relationship you could work on this week.

3. New immigrants are coming to our communities every day. If there is such a group, or even just one family, make an effort to help them become established in their homes, the schools, and the community at large. Offer to adopt a new family in need; provide support and encouragement.

Invitation to Closing Prayer

Give thanks to God (aloud or silently) for his very presence in the world. Conclude with the following:

Lord our God,
thank you for bringing us
into the love relationship
that exists in your being from all eternity.

We humbly offer you ourselves in return,
and ask that you use us as you will
in the work set before us.

As you embrace us in solidarity,
help us to embrace those around us
who are alone
and in need of your living presence.

We offer this prayer,
in the name of the Father,
and of the Son,
and of the Holy Spirit. Amen.

THE MOST HOLY BODY AND BLOOD OF CHRIST

The Body of Christ

Invitation to Pray

Pause for a few moments of silence and enter more deeply into the presence of God.

Opening Song
Now We Remain

Proclaim the Gospel

Luke 9:11b-17
Feeding of the Five Thousand

Take a few minutes to savor a word, a phrase, a question, or a feeling that rises up in you. Reflect on this quietly or share it aloud.

The other Scripture readings of the day are
Genesis 14:18-20,
Psalm 110:1-4,
and 1 Corinthians 11:23-26.

Invitation to Reflect on the Gospel

This Gospel presents us with another example of Jesus' efforts to encourage the disciples to think differently about what is possible in a seemingly impossible situation. The feeding of the multitude is connected with Jesus' preaching about the reign of God and his healing all those in need of healing. The disciples readily accept what Jesus taught about the reign of God as well as the healing miracles. Perhaps this is because they were observers, and not actively involved in the preaching and healing.

However, when the disciples expressed concern about the lateness of the day and the peoples' need for food and lodging, Jesus challenges them to participate in the work of a miracle: his words are forceful and direct: "Give them some food yourselves" (v. 13). They are not able to see that the little they have, the five loaves and two fish, is more than enough when it is offered faithfully, humbly, and with gratitude. So it is with us. As members of the Church, we are called to think differently about who we are and what we have to offer.

Similar to Trinity Sunday, the Feast of the Body and Blood of Christ is the celebration of mystery: the mystery of the bread and wine becoming Jesus in the Eucharist, and the mystery of the Church as the Body of Christ here on earth. Jesus foreshadows the institution of the Eucharist in the feeding of the multitude: he takes the food, looks to heaven, blesses the food, breaks it, and gives it. In receiving Communion, we come into union with God in Jesus Christ and we are united to each other; we are made into the Body of Christ. We are not merely observers any longer; we are participants in the working of this mystery. In symbols of bread and wine, we offer our life; in the Body and Blood of Jesus, we offer again Christ's sacrifice to the Father. Nourished by the Eucharist, we become the food, the presence of God, for those who are broken, lonely, and hungry in our community.

Invitation to Group Sharing

1. What impact does the real presence of Jesus in the Eucharist have on my life? How has the meaning of Eucharist deepened since my First Communion?

2. How do I prepare to receive the Body and Blood of Christ? What are my thoughts while receiving? What goes on in my prayer after I receive Communion?

3. How can I share with others what Eucharist means to me? How can we help others to appreciate the incredible significance of Jesus being truly present in the Eucharist?

Invitation to Act

Determine a specific action (individual or group) that flows from your sharing. This should be your primary consideration. When choosing an individual action, determine what you will do and share it with the group. When choosing a group action, determine who will take responsibility for different aspects of the action. The following are secondary suggestions:

1. The next time you receive the Eucharist, be deliberate in your "Amen!" when presented with the Body and Blood of Christ. Amen means more than "I believe" or "so it is." It means "I ratify and confirm in my life what I believe." Be conscious about what you are saying.

2. If you serve as a eucharistic minister, try to spend some quiet time before the Blessed Sacrament as a way to be refreshed in your ministry.

3. Contact the pastor or someone else in pastoral leadership in your parish and ask for the name of someone who is homebound who might appreciate being visited a couple times a month, in addition to

the regular Communion call. Gather some volunteers to do the same for others.

4. Sometimes hospitals have volunteer "baby-holders" for babies who are hospital-bound for extended periods. If your local hospital has such a program, consider volunteering for a couple hours once a month.

Invitation to Closing Prayer

Give thanks to God (aloud or silently) for giving us Jesus, the Bread of Life. Conclude with the following:

Heavenly Father,
thank you for giving us yourself
in Jesus,
through the Eucharist.

As we are fed by you,
open our eyes to see those who are hungry, lonely,
and in need of your presence.
By the grace of your Spirit,
may we live as the Body of Christ.

With grateful hearts,
we offer the gifts we have
so that we may become bread
for the life of the world.

In Jesus' name we pray. Amen.

SEASON OF THE YEAR

(Ordinary Time)

SECOND SUNDAY IN ORDINARY TIME

Image of God in Life

Invitation to Pray

Pause for a few moments of silence and enter more deeply into the presence of God.

Opening Song
We Shall Draw Water

Proclaim the Gospel

John 2:1-11
The Wedding Feast at Cana

Take a few minutes to savor a word, a phrase, a question, or a feeling that rises up in you. Reflect on this quietly or share it aloud.

The other Scripture readings of the day are

Isaiah 62:1-5,
Psalm 96:1-3, 7-10,
and 1 Corinthians 12:4-11.

Invitation to Reflect on the Gospel

In the wedding feast of Cana we see Jesus pressed by his mother's compassion to respond to a social dilemma. It was a wedding feast, a primal social event within the local community. Marriage bound the community together by linking families through relationships of longevity. The social fabric of the community was strengthened by the celebrations of these unions. It was proper and fitting to celebrate with everyone present.

How embarrassing to miscalculate the needed amount of wine or to be unable to afford the quantity that would allow people to celebrate this major covenantal event! Whatever the circumstances, Mary noted the problem and approached the one person whom she knew could alleviate the discomfort. We have no idea what she thought Jesus would do, but we do know that she felt confident in asking him for help. While Jesus resists the appeal initially, like the good son who relents and responds fully in the parable of the two sons (Matthew 21:28-32), he proceeds to respectfully honor her request.

This is not a statement about familial control or God being subject to any human preference. It is a story that depicts Jesus as a man who cared about the needs of those around him. In everyday life, Jesus could be moved to respond in order to meet people where they were. Mary knew this capacity in her Son. She trusted him to reach out and alleviate the struggle in some way. Of course, he made this miracle a sign of his "hour," giving it a profound meaning that Mary would come to understand.

God is concerned about human dilemmas and limitations and chooses to respond. Our petitions, spoken from the depths of surrendered hearts, aware of their dependency upon a generous God, fall upon God's ears and receive a hearing. While we may not know the precise way in which God will respond, we can be assured the voices that cry out are heard.

Invitation to Group Sharing

1. Do I feel confident enough of God's attentiveness in my everyday life that I speak out my needs in prayer or trust some response will be given?

2. When have I experienced the outpouring of God's generous response in my life?

3. When we look back on the past year, how have we as a community witnessed God's concrete response to our real needs?

4. What needs have we, as a community, *not* yet placed before God to seek guidance?

Invitation to Act

Determine a specific action (individual or group) that flows from your sharing. This should be your primary consideration. When choosing an individual action, determine what you will do and share it with the group. When choosing a group action, determine who will take responsibility for different aspects of the action. The following are secondary suggestions:

1. As a group, formulate a support system for newlyweds and/or new parents to help them adjust to the demands of their circumstances.

2. Provide some assistance to young couples, for instance, through sharing your story and listening to theirs, or babysitting. If you are able, you might consider offering financial subsidies, or interest-free loans that alleviate some of the real tensions in their situations.

3. Set up a team in your parish to help engaged couples participate in an Engaged Encounter, providing letters of support, prayer cards, and a welcome gathering upon their return to talk about their experience.

Invitation to Closing Prayer

Give thanks to God (aloud or silently) for insights gained, for desires awakened, for directions clarified, for the gift of one another's openness and sensitivity. Conclude with the following, read as a litany by a leader with responses by the group.

Leader   For the times, Lord, when we have resisted responding to the needs of those who are beginning life anew:

we say, "Lord, have mercy."

All   **Lord, have mercy.**

Leader   For the times when we have neglected to reach out because we were preoccupied with our own lives and failed to recognize the vulnerability of another:

we say, "Christ, have mercy."

All   **Christ, have mercy.**

Leader   For the times when we have failed to prevent the shaming of another through acts of protective concern, charity, or sharing our resources:

we say, "Lord, have mercy."

All   **Lord, have mercy.**

Leader   We surrender to you, God of great generosity.

Guide our actions, our attitudes, and our attentiveness so that we may discern when to say "yes" to your call through those who struggle around us.

We pray this in Jesus' name.

All   **Amen.**

Third Sunday
in Ordinary Time

Power of the Spirit Gives Jesus Authority

Invitation to Pray

Pause for a few moments of silence and enter more deeply into the presence of God.

Opening Song
We Are Called
or
God Has Chosen Me

Proclaim the Gospel
Luke 1:1-4; 4:14-21
Jesus First Preaches in Nazareth

Take a few minutes to savor a word, a phrase, a question, or a feeling that rises up in you. Reflect on this quietly or share it aloud.

The other Scripture readings of the day are

Nehemiah 8:2-4a, 5-6, 8-10,
Psalm 19:8-10, 15,
and 1 Corinthians 12:12-30.

Invitation to Reflect on the Gospel

Today's Gospel reading is the wonderful account of Jesus' ministerial debut in Nazareth, his hometown. He chooses for his first sermon the beautiful text from Isaiah that speaks of a heavenly transformation of the earth; a prophetic prediction of a world where liberty is brought to captives and recovery of sight is given to those who cannot see. The Spirit of God empowers him to speak prophetically and authoritatively.

Luke is writing for a Gentile Christian community. Whereas the Hebrew Christians were familiar with the prophetic tradition of Isaiah, the Gentiles were not privy to this in their background.

This citation of Isaiah was a radical new concept to their religious sensibilities. Luke tells us how he systematically compiled data to be included in a Gospel version that was pertinent to his non-Hebraic listeners. He documents his narrative sources and, then, stretches his audience with the social ramifications of Jesus' call.

We are equally stretched by the prophetic images to which Jesus refers. He takes a messianic text and reveals his identity through it. He speaks of fulfillment in a world where inequities still exist. What challenge does this place upon us as we live our lives as family members and individuals within a larger society?

In our time, we must grapple with continuing the implementation of Jesus' mandate. Let us visit the text again and derive a contemporary meaning for ourselves. As followers, we are challenged to promote the legacy of anointing the world, bringing glad tidings to those who are impoverished in body, mind, spirit, or social consequence. Like the Gentile believers, we must take up afresh the message so that Jesus' proclamation is realized by those who live in our day. Then, we, too, can boldly announce that "Today this scripture passage is fulfilled in your hearing" (v. 4:21).

Invitation to Group Sharing

1. How do I participate in bringing "glad tidings to the poor" and proclaiming "liberty to captives"?

2. How am I (or we as a group) being stretched in understanding Christ's mandate to help in the recovery of sight to the blind and the release of prisoners, that is, those who are in need?

3. What can we as a group do to respond more wholeheartedly to realize the fulfillment of these instructions?

Invitation to Act

Determine a specific action (individual or group) that flows from your sharing. This should be your primary consideration. When choosing an individual action, determine what you will do and share it with the group. When choosing a group action, determine who will take responsibility for different aspects of the action. The following are secondary suggestions:

1. Begin or join an outreach process to those in prison, corresponding with them, visiting them or their families, and advocating for justice where injustice has been found. Consider being a partner in prayer and in reconciliation with a prisoner.

2. Become involved in supporting those who oppose abortion. Contact your diocesan Respect Life Office for information.

3. Become informed about capital punishment, listening as a group to the challenge of mercy and how best to respond in a Gospel spirit. In response to that reflection and awareness, consider involvement with those who are on death row.

4. Encourage the visit and inclusion of persons with disabilities to your parish and facilitate their access to your buildings, worship, and special events.

5. Make a donation to Catholic Charities or volunteer to help at a local soup kitchen.

Invitation to Closing Prayer

*Give thanks to God (aloud or silently) for insights
gained, for desires awakened, for directions clarified,
for the gift of one another's openness and sensitivity.*

Conclude with the following:

God of our hopes and our dreams,
you have planted the hunger for "glad tidings" within us.

Make our joy more complete
as we participate
in proclaiming this Good News;
the blind will see,
the prisoner will be released.

Give us the courage
to reach out to the incarcerated
and bring into reality
this promise of freedom.

Help us to diffuse our fears
and know how to realize our call
so that "a year acceptable"
may be celebrated in your name.

We pray this,
holding our reservations and anxiety up to you,
and we ask for your blessing and grace,
through Jesus Christ our Lord,
and through your Holy Spirit. Amen.

FOURTH SUNDAY IN ORDINARY TIME

The Church's Mission Is the Option for the Poor

Invitation to Pray

Pause for a few moments of silence and enter more deeply into the presence of God.

Opening Song

God Has Chosen Me

Proclaim the Gospel

Luke 4:21-30
Jesus Cast Out of Nazareth

Take a few minutes to savor a word, a phrase, a question, or a feeling that rises up in you. Reflect on this quietly or share it aloud.

The other Scripture readings of the day are

Jeremiah 1:4-5, 17-19,
Psalm 71:1-6, 15, 17,
and 1 Corinthians 12:31—13:13.

Invitation to Reflect on the Gospel

From within our own families, communities, and marriages, it is often difficult to hear a challenging or "prophetic" word. These are the people with whom we live. We know their weaknesses and vulnerabilities. They know ours. To be stretched into a new level of responsibility by those with whom we live and on whom we depend is a very uncomfortable experience. We would prefer to appear perfect in their eyes, without need of change, improvement, or challenge.

Today we witness Jesus' struggle with the same phenomenon. His reading of Isaiah stresses the social dimension of God's call to Israel, a message that challenges comfortable lifestyles, attitudinal biases, and the status quo. Members of his own community rebel. Who is he to play the prophet? Is he not just a "regular guy" who should pay attention to his own life and not interfere in others' lives?

The prophetic call has left many a challenger on the margins of society, abandoned and derided by the complacent. Many missionaries have come home with news of needs beyond the borders of their home countries and have been met with indifference, discomfort, and dismissal. The reaction of Jesus' compatriots was even stronger; they wanted to throw him off the hill.

In our relationships with our family members, our Christian commitment is often severely challenged. We must take care that our efforts to renew the human family do not detract from the time and energy that should be given to our own spouses and children.

But the prophetic call is perennial. So, too, is the prophetic response; as pertinent today as in Jesus' day, it is one that moves us to share our treasures with those who are in need. Our prophetic response may be as difficult as the prophet's call itself. To tailor our lifestyle around our awareness that a global world must live on limited resources can raise suspicion, ridicule, and criticism. Witnessing to a simpler way of living may be as uncomfortable as directly speaking the challenge to others. Equally prophetic, it may take us to the brink of the hill, to the edge of society. But we will have companionship. In all that it entails, we will share the comfort that Christ is there walking alongside us through the rejection to another level of freedom and fullness.

Invitation to Group Sharing

1. What current news events have recently raised awareness of my need to react with a courageous response?

2. When have I experienced the tension of the "prophet" in trying to introduce greater involvement with and commitment to those who are poor or with any unpopular stand?

3. What are the "prophetic" and/or positive stands our group has taken in following the Gospel? If we have not taken any, what might be hindering us?

Invitation to Act

Determine a specific action (individual or group) that flows from your sharing. This should be your primary consideration. When choosing an individual action, determine what you will do and share it with the group. When choosing a group action, determine who will take responsibility for different aspects of the action. The following are secondary suggestions:

1. Determine to address an unjust situation you may be witnessing in the circumstances of your daily life.

2. Invite a returned missionary or someone working with people or populations who are marginalized to visit and speak of the social challenges their work raises for you as a parish family.

3. Adopt a particular mission community and pledge financial support to enable its projects and good works to continue.

4. Link up with an organization that provides services
    to refugees, and design a plan of involvement with a
    family in transition. Hold a potluck dinner for that
    family so they can meet others from your parish.

Invitation to Closing Prayer

*Give thanks to God (aloud or silently) for insights gained,
for desires awakened, for directions clarified, for the gift of
one another's openness and sensitivity. Conclude with the
following:*

Holy One of Israel,
you were rebuffed by your loved ones,
who would not receive the prophet's call through you.

We ache with your rejection.

We want to hear the challenges of Isaiah today
and respond wholeheartedly,
despite our fears of what this call may require.

We place ourselves at your disposal.

Direct us to the needs you would have us address,
so that your kingdom on earth comes into being,
now and forevermore. Amen.

FIFTH SUNDAY IN ORDINARY TIME

Peter's Call to Discipleship

Invitation to Pray

Pause for a few moments of silence and enter more deeply into the presence of God.

Opening Song
Lord, You Have Come

Proclaim the Gospel

Luke 5:1-11
Jesus Calls Peter

Take a few minutes to savor a word, a phrase, a question, or a feeling that rises up in you. Reflect on this quietly or share it aloud.

The other Scripture readings of the day are

Isaiah 6:1-2a, 3-8,
Psalm 138:1-8,
and 1 Corinthians 15:1-11.

Invitation to Reflect on the Gospel

None of us is worthy of the call of God. Who God calls into service or how God intends to reveal the kingdom to the world through them has little to do with worthiness. Certainly, throughout the Scriptures, Peter reveals again and again how clumsy he was with the invitation of God and how imperfect a choice he was for doing great things. Yet, that did not prevent Jesus from calling him into radical service and leadership, nor did it ultimately inhibit miracles from happening for Peter's benefit and edification.

What *is* a significant factor in receiving the call of God is willingness. This willingness is one that allows us to set out into the deep in our relationship with God and be transformed from that depth. Certainly, we resonate with Peter's hesitancy. Like Peter, we may be incredulous at the call. At times, we may experience the call of God as daunting in its consequences. Peter's life radically changed when he let Jesus into his boat to catch that startling load of fish. His awareness of his own inadequacy made him want to push Jesus away and refute the call. However, something deep within him was stirred by this encounter with Christ and he willingly consented to follow Jesus.

The call involves a willingness to risk. It requires an openness to being surprised by God. In saying "yes" to that invitation, Peter embraced a life that was beyond his wildest dreams. He experienced a relationship of intimacy with Jesus that would definitively shift his priorities and his lifestyle.

Like Peter, we risk realizing our own greatness when we say "yes" to God in Christ. We enter into a partnership, a discipleship, when we consent to God's invitation. We bring to the call humility and an awareness that nothing great can happen of our own doing. It may be necessary for God to reach out and perform minor miracles to convince us that the call is real. We may require some purification in order to be ready. It may take a miraculous catch of some kind to help us realize God's seriousness. But our call is as real as Peter's, and so is the risk. Are we willing?

Invitation to Group Sharing

1. How do I sense God's call and respond to it?

2. To what do I feel God is now calling me and how do I intend to respond?

3. As a group, what are some of the common elements of our call to discipleship (that is, our call to follow Jesus)? For instance, desire for God, willingness to listen and obey, fear of consequences, etc.

4. What have been the most rewarding aspects of having said, "yes"?

Invitation to Act

Determine a specific action (individual or group) that flows from your sharing. This should be your primary consideration. When choosing an individual action, determine what you will do and share it with the group. When choosing a group action, determine who will take responsibility for different aspects of the action. The following are secondary suggestions:

1. Examine the parish's attention to and support of vocations to ministry—lay, clerical, and religious—and formulate deliberate ways to raise awareness; for example, inquiry retreats, conversations, sponsorships. Contact your Diocesan Office of Vocations for ideas and assistance.

2. Be involved in a the program which encourages lay ministry in the parish. Establish a scholarship for laity who seek to enter studies for ministry.

3. Make it a daily practice to pray for priestly and religious vocations and encourage the practice in the parish.

4. Dedicate a time of prayer this week to reflect on your call to discipleship. Be open to the newness of life that Jesus offers you.

Invitation to Closing Prayer

Give thanks to God (aloud or silently) for insights gained, for desires awakened, for directions clarified, for the gift of one another's openness and sensitivity. Conclude with the following:

Jesus, brother and Lord,
your call to Peter
is echoed in our own calls to discipleship.

At times we feel unsure
of how you could possibly desire us
for this service.

Yet, we know you can do great things with our lives
if only we consent.

Take our hesitancy and our reticence
and transform them into courage and confidence in you.

Teach us how to respond wholeheartedly
to your invitation
and move more deeply
into intimate relationship with you.

We say "yes" to serving you and your people
in truth, justice, and mercy.

We pray this in your name. Amen.

SIXTH SUNDAY IN ORDINARY TIME

Discipleship's Challenge

Invitation to Pray

Pause for a few moments of silence and enter more deeply into the presence of God.

Opening Song
Peace, My Friends

Proclaim the Gospel

Luke 6:17, 20-26
Ministering to a Great Multitude

Take a few minutes to savor a word, a phrase, a question, or a feeling that rises up in you. Reflect on this quietly or share it aloud.

The other Scripture readings of the day are
Jeremiah 17:5-8,
Psalm 1:1-4, 6, and
1 Corinthians 15:12,16-20.

Invitation to Reflect on the Gospel

Luke's version of the Beatitudes has a more challenging bite to it than Matthew's. In Luke, we get the "woes" as well as the "blesseds" and some find the woes a little frightening:

"But woe to you who are rich,
for you have received your consolation.

But woe to you who are filled now,
for you will be hungry" (v. 24-25).

For those of us who are considered relatively rich and filled by the world's standards, this Gospel is a real challenge. It presents a counter-cultural lifestyle that seems foolish at best and self-destructive at worst.

But while Jesus' "upside-down" way of thinking and living may seem foolish, it is anything but self-destructive. In fact, it's just the opposite. As Jesus continually reminds us, those who save their lives will lose them and those who lose their lives for his sake and the sake of the Gospel will find them (see Mark 8:35).

So here we are, many of us, considered relatively rich, filled, and well-thought of by many. What are we supposed to do? This is not an easy question to answer.

Jesus seems to be challenging those of us with riches and privileges to go further. The rich young man was asked by Jesus to give all his riches to the poor and then follow him. Francis of Assisi took this literally and became a saint. Jesus is challenging all of us—individually, as a family, as a parish family, and as the Church. We cannot serve two masters.

We have a unique opportunity to give away at least some of our riches, our privileges, and even some of our titles or positions, and embrace Jesus' and Francis' path of simplicity of life. Giving away money and goods could involve drawing up an inventory of all our things, giving away all but essentials. Or it could mean adopting an "exchange system" according to which something is given away whenever something similar is purchased, for example, clothes, appliances, toys, or games. Giving away privileges requires much more imagination. Those of us who are male can defer to women in situations where men are often deferred to. Those of us in positions of authority can seek ways of serving those who are accustomed to serving us. Every day is truly an opportunity for justice and freedom.

Invitation to Group Sharing

1. To what extent am I one of those who is privileged, rich, filled, and well-thought of?

2. Considering benefits I may have in my lifestyle, what can I do to be more sensitive to those less privileged?

3. What changes in my lifestyle is Jesus asking me and my faith community to make today?

Invitation to Act

Determine a specific action (individual or group) that flows from your sharing. This should be your primary consideration. When choosing an individual action, determine what you will do and share it with the group. When choosing a group action, determine who will take responsibility for different aspects of the action. The following are secondary suggestions:

1. Consider how your lifestyle might better respond to the challenge Jesus offers in this Gospel.

2. Reach out compassionately to someone in your life who is hungry, weeping, hated, or excluded. Remember him or her in your daily prayer. Commit to one conversation this week with this person face-to-face or on the telephone.

3. Identify some group in your community that is particularly hurting and decide how to respond; for example, sponsor an immigrant family who might otherwise be a victim to the anti-immigration sentiment in this country.

Invitation to Closing Prayer

Give thanks to God (aloud or silently) for insights gained, for desires awakened, for directions clarified, for the gift of one another's openness and sensitivity. Conclude with the following (recite aloud together):

Jesus, once again you comfort the afflicted
and afflict the comfortable.

Help us continue to open ourselves
to your challenging word and witness.

Give us the courage to make hard decisions
about our lifestyle and
the compassion to embrace those who are
hurting in our families and community.

And let us never forget that your grace is sufficient.

You will never ask of us more than we can give.

And you will always be walking with us
in the process.

This we ask in your name, Jesus Christ,
you, who live and reign with God our Father
in the unity of the Holy Spirit, now and forever. Amen.

SEVENTH SUNDAY IN ORDINARY TIME

Love Your Enemies

Invitation to Pray

Pause for a few moments of silence and enter more deeply into the presence of God.

Opening Song

The Prayer of St. Francis
(Make Me a Channel of Your Peace)

Proclaim the Gospel

Luke 6:27-38
Debates about the Sabbath

Take a few minutes to savor a word, a phrase, a question, or a feeling that rises up in you. Reflect on this quietly or share it aloud.

The other Scripture readings of the day are

1 Samuel 26:2, 7-9, 12-13, 22-23,
Psalm 103:1-4, 8, 10, 12-13,
and 1 Corinthians 15:45-49.

Invitation to Reflect on the Gospel

Nothing in the Gospel is more difficult than this—to love our enemies, to do good to those who mistreat us, to lend without any expectation of return. Jesus became our model for such unconditional love and mercy when he was being nailed to a cross. But how easy it is, how "natural" some would say, to want to retaliate against those who have hurt us.

We find this tendency in our personal lives, even in our homes. We want to get even with others. If our children hurt us in some way, even just by being ungrateful, we sometimes find ourselves saying (or at least thinking) "That's the last favor I'll do for you!" or, "Just wait until the next time you want me to do something for you!" But God's mercy challenges us to a much higher standard. And then there's that frightening phrase in the Lord's Prayer when we ask God to forgive us in the same way that we forgive others!

In routine interactions with others, we have lots of opportunities to practice this demanding imperative. There are those unfriendly salespersons or customers, waiters who are not as attentive to our needs as we would like, passers-by who do not respond to our cheerful greeting, and drivers who irritate us on the highway. Will it be our best self or our worst self that responds? Each of these encounters, as well as the family ones, are opportunities to become more like Jesus who was able to say by the end of his earthly life: "Father, forgive them, they know not what they do" (Luke 23:34).

Unfortunately, when we look at societal practices, we see an escalating retaliation that affects us all. From the sports arena (where players often "have to" retaliate or be benched) to the criminal justice system (in some states capital punishment seems to be more popular than ever), forgiveness or leniency is regarded as weakness. But God has provided powerful counter witnesses of mercy, people like Sr. Helen Prejean and those involved in "Victim-Offender Reconciliation Programs" (VORP), who show us how to embrace the perpetrators as well as the victims of crime. The heroic witness of Nelson Mandela and Archbishop Desmond Tutu in South Africa, of Anne Frank, Etty Hillesum, and other forgiving victims of the

Holocaust can inspire us Christians to put the heroic love of Jesus and the infinite mercy of God into practice in our own time and situations.

Invitation to Group Sharing

1. What kinds of situations in life tend to trigger people's desire to retaliate?

2. What examples of forgiveness and/or retaliation have I encountered in society (or at home) that have touched or disturbed me recently?

3. Is there one person with whom I could offer forgiveness over retaliation or choose kindness over hostility?

4. How can I, individually, and we, as a faith community, address the need to promote love or rehabilitation over hostility and retaliation in the wider community?

Invitation to Act

Determine a specific action (individual or group) that flows from your sharing. This should be your primary consideration. When choosing an individual action, determine what you will do and share it with the group. When choosing a group action, determine who will take responsibility for different aspects of the action. The following are secondary suggestions:

1. Pray about, and talk over with your spouse or a trusted friend, situations where you experience ingratitude and find yourself wanting to pull back rather than love more freely. Write a prayer to the Lord asking for patience to love more freely. Carry this in your pocket, wallet, or purse this week.

2. Identify some family or friendship situation that needs healing and take a first step toward reconciliation by reaching out to that person in a positive way, perhaps acknowledging your own sinfulness in the situation. Pray over the situation first, asking for inspiration from the Holy Spirit.

3. Examine how you react in competitive situations, especially in sports, cards, or other games, and resolve never to "get even" and to discourage others from doing so as well. Find a "cold water word" or phrase or gesture for cooling off situations that are beginning to overheat.

4. Raise within your faith community or civic community the issue of capital punishment and/or other highly punitive responses to social problems. Perhaps invite a member of Victim-Offender Reconciliation Program (VORP) to speak to your group(s). Consult: www.vorp.com

Invitation to Closing Prayer

Give thanks to God (aloud or silently) for insights gained, for desires awakened, for directions clarified, for the gift of one another's openness and sensitivity. Conclude with the following (recite aloud together):

Jesus,
your witness of unconditional love and forgiveness
is really difficult to follow.
Please help us as we struggle.
Do not let us become discouraged.
Help us to get back up each time we fail,
and to resolve more firmly
to be merciful and forgiving as you were.

Help us to realize each day
that you have sent your Spirit of Love
to inhabit our heart,
and to call on that Holy Spirit
each time we feel
the fires of resentment and retaliation
building up inside.
Transform our hostile hearts.
Transform our hostile society. Amen.

Eighth Sunday in Ordinary Time

Jesus Is Our Master Teacher; We Are His Disciples

Invitation to Pray

Pause for a few moments of silence and enter more deeply into the presence of God.

Opening Song

God of Day and God of Darkness

Proclaim the Gospel

Luke 6:39-45
Judging Others

Take a few minutes to savor a word, a phrase, a question, or a feeling that rises up in you. Reflect on this quietly or share it aloud.

The other Scripture readings of the day are

Sirach 27:4-7,
Psalm 92:2-3, 13-16,
and 1 Corinthians 15:54-58.

Invitation to Reflect on the Gospel

Many of us would find it difficult to answer the question, "who are you and what do you do?" with, "I'm a Christian, a disciple of Christ." Peter couldn't do it. In fact, three times he denied even knowing Jesus. We are much more comfortable with conventional responses like, "I'm a teacher, a bus driver, a homemaker, a parent." Rarely do we see our fundamental identity as being a follower or disciple of Jesus. If asked who was our favorite teacher or who is our favorite religious author or spiritual guide, how many of us would say "Jesus"? Francis of Assisi was so concerned about the penchant for studying theology under the masters and the pride that often comes with academic credentials, that he forbade his followers from reading any other book than the Bible. Jesus should be our master teacher.

Unfortunately in our secular society, there is an overabundance of gurus and goods to pursue, many of them counter to the Way of Jesus. Because of the power of advertising, they are even more seductive. One commercial for a brokerage house used the desire for wealth to try to allure us this way: "When [the C.E.O.] speaks, everyone listens." Imagine if the message of Jesus could claim such a rating. Unfortunately, many people, including those who call themselves Christians, long for someone who can give them comforting messages, make things seem simple. Many of these "cultural evangelists" turn out to be the "blind leading the blind" down the path of possessions, power, prestige, and privileges. Jesus desperately needs his disciples to be just that, his disciples, teachers of his Word and Way, prophets in the situations and circles where we live and work and volunteer.

As apprentice teachers and prophets, we learn our "script" first of all by studying the Scriptures, as St. Francis of Assisi and the other saints did. We grow further in our trade by listening carefully to our master in silent prayer and frequent reception of Jesus in the Eucharist. As John the Baptist realized, so must we: that Jesus must increase and we must decrease (see John 3:30). We learn our master's priorities and encounter him further when we reach out compassionately to those he embraced—people who are forgotten and marginalized.

As we grow through this "on the job training," it is very helpful to have other disciples with whom to serve and reflect. A spiritual director, a small faith-sharing or prayer group, and a vibrant faith community can all help us to recognize the false prophets and idols around us, and to discern where and how best to be teachers and prophets for Jesus. We can pick one another up when we grow weary or face difficult situations.

Invitation to Group Sharing

1. What societal messages and worldly goods tempt me the most?

2. What kinds of things tend to keep me from being bolder about living and proclaiming my Christian faith?

3. What kinds of changes do I, and we as a faith community, need to make, to learn, live, and teach the Way of Jesus?

4. What one step can I as an individual, and we as a faith community, take to become more committed disciples, teachers, and prophets for Jesus?

Invitation to Act

Determine a specific action (individual or group) that flows from your sharing. This should be your primary consideration. When choosing an individual action, determine what you will do and share it with the group. When choosing a group action, determine who will take responsibility for different aspects of the action. The following are secondary suggestions:

1. Set aside time each day for prayerful reading and/or listening to the Word of God in Scripture.

2. Read the life of a saintly disciple and prophet of Jesus. Contemporary people like Dorothy Day, Oscar

Romero, Blessed Mother Teresa, and Martin Luther King, Jr. help us to critique the seductiveness of an affluent society, as well as reveal the meaning of prophetic living.

3. Find a spiritual director and/or become part of a small faith-sharing or ministry group to help you discern and live the Word and Way of Jesus in the midst of a seductive culture.

4. Choose one area of your life where you can experiment regularly in being a bolder teacher and prophet for Christ. Do something similar as a faith community.

Invitation to Closing Prayer

Give thanks to God (aloud or silently) for insights gained, for desires awakened, for directions clarified, for the gift of one another's openness and sensitivity. Conclude with the following (recite aloud together):

Jesus,
it is hard to comprehend just how privileged we are.

You have chosen us as your students, your disciples,
and you want us to fully mature
as teachers of your Word and Way.

No matter what our job, our career,
and the daily tasks we embrace,
you want us to follow your Way
and represent you in every encounter we have.

Please help us spend some of our best time each day
getting to know you better.

Help us learn how to love as you loved
and be the instruments of your love to others.

This we ask in your name, you who live and reign
with the Father, and the Holy Spirit,
world without end. Amen.

NINTH SUNDAY IN ORDINARY TIME

The Faith That Heals

Invitation to Pray

Pause for a few moments of silence and enter more deeply into the presence of God.

Opening Song

Sing to the Mountains
or Leaning on the Everlasting Arms

Proclaim the Gospel

Luke 7:1-10
Healing of a Centurion's Slave

Take a few minutes to savor a word, a phrase, a question, or a feeling that rises up in you. Reflect on this quietly or share it aloud.

The other Scripture readings of the day are

1 Kings 8:41-43,
Psalm 117:1-2,
and Galatians 1:1-2, 6-10.)

Invitation to Reflect on the Gospel

Jesus was truly amazed at the combination of faith and love he found in the Roman centurion. The centurion's faith in the powerful love of God embodied in the person of Jesus to heal his servant was so evident that he simply asked Jesus to "say the word" (v. 7). But the centurion's love for his servant also impressed Jesus, for servants and slaves were clearly not highly regarded in Jesus' time.

When we pray with a similar combination of faith and love, we should expect similar results. Unfortunately, however, many of us have not developed these virtues as much as the centurion had. If we truly believed that GOD *is love* (1 John 4:8) and he loves every creature, including ourselves, with measureless love, we would find ourselves sounding more and more like the centurion.

Sometimes it's desperation as much as faith that brings us to our knees begging for help. I remember all too clearly the desperation I experienced years ago in the midst of a serious depression. The words that came daily from the depths of my being were those familiar eucharistic words: "Lord, I am not worthy to receive you, but only say the word and I shall be healed." Jesus wants us to discover what he knew—just how loving God is. Jesus gave us the Eucharist as a way of being totally available to us every day, not just to walk into our homes but to walk into our very being.

There are ways to develop the faith of the centurion, so that we will be able to recognize and embrace Jesus as he comes to us each day, ready to heal us in little ways and sometimes in dramatic ways. We can begin by setting aside time each day to listen and speak with Jesus in prayer. We can accept his invitation to receive him more frequently in Communion. We can become part of a faith-filled small Christian community and/or worshipping community. Those members of my own parish who have witnessed and prayed with our pastor as he lays his healing hands on those who are ill have grown tremendously in their own faith and love.

But it is for more than personal healing that Jesus wants us to pray and work. It is for the healing of our society and world. Here is where so many of us despair of being able to do anything to embrace the familiar words of the Lord's Prayer: "Your kingdom come, your will be done on earth as it is in heaven" (Matthew 6:10). In the face of escalating violence and massive injustice, many give up and retreat into their private worlds and private prayers. Many others, however, dare to believe as Jesus did, that if they allow their seed to fall into the ground and die in service to others, it will bear much fruit. In the words of a favorite Gospel spiritual in our faith community: "If we had faith the size of a mustard seed, we'd say 'move, mountain; move, mountain; mountain, get outta my way!'"

Invitation to Group Sharing

1. What are some of the obstacles that keep me from becoming a person of deep faith and love, like the centurion?

2. In what ways do I intend to deepen my faith?

3. What specific persons or situations in my life need healing and how can I escalate my prayerful pleading on their behalf?

4. How can we as a faith community encourage and practice the combination of faith and love we see in the centurion?

Invitation to Act

Determine a specific action (individual or group) that flows from your sharing. This should be your primary consideration. When choosing an individual action, determine what you will do and share it with the group. When choosing a group action, determine who will take responsibility for different aspects of the action. The following are secondary suggestions:

1. Cultivate an awareness of God's presence and action in your lives and world by identifying regularly the ways you have experienced God and God's many gifts that day. This can and should be done alone,

with a spouse or close friend, and occasionally as part of a support group.

2. Cultivate the practice of daily prayers for physical and spiritual healings for specific persons and offer up some sacrificial actions (what Cursillo calls *palanca*) on their behalf. We will be acting ourselves into a new way of thinking and believing.

3. Contact a local organization that serves people with AIDS and see if your group can provide meals, help with childcare, take care of household chores, etc. Be a friend to someone with AIDS; be with them in their suffering.

Invitation to Closing Prayer

Give thanks to God (aloud or silently) for insights gained, for desires awakened, for directions clarified, for the gift of one another's openness and sensitivity. Conclude with the following (recite aloud together):

God of mercy and justice,
you give us so many examples of your healing presence
in Scripture, in our daily lives, and in the events of history.

Thank you for the incredible gift of your presence
in the person of Jesus
and his intimate union with us through the Eucharist.

How lavish your love is!

We acknowledge and confess our lack of faith,
our lack of love, and our lack of courage
for being your instruments of healing in our own time.

Open our eyes, deepen our faith.

Send us your Spirit of love and courage
to pray and work for the healing
of suffering individuals in our lives
and for the healing of our suffering society and world.

We ask this in the name of Jesus Christ our Lord. Amen.

TENTH SUNDAY IN ORDINARY TIME

Are We Moved to Pity or Do We Blame?

Invitation to Pray

Pause for a few moments of silence and enter more deeply into the presence of God.

Opening Song
Whatsoever You Do

Proclaim the Gospel
Luke 7:11-17
Raising of the Widow's Son

Take a few minutes to savor a word, a phrase, a question, or a feeling that rises up in you. Reflect on this quietly or share it aloud.

The other Scripture readings of the day are

1 Kings 17:17-24,
Psalm 30:2, 4-6, 11-13,
and Galatians 1:11-19.

Invitation to Reflect on the Gospel

Jesus was moved with compassion. It was as simple as that. When he saw the grieving widow and mother, he did not ask about her economic status, about her moral behavior, or even her religion. He saw her suffering and responded immediately and wholeheartedly.

Wonderful witness exists of a young disciple of Jesus named Trevor Farrell. At age eleven, Trevor was watching the TV news one evening and saw a news clip about those who are homeless in Philadelphia. With great persistence, he talked his father into driving him that same evening through areas where those who are homeless hang out. At a stop light along the way, Trevor impulsively jumped out of the car and gave the pillow and blanket he had brought with him to a man sleeping on the streets. From that first night until the day he graduated from high school, Trevor did not miss a night on the streets! Eventually Trevor became "Trevor's Campaign": feeding hundreds of people nightly out of a traveling van; opening a temporary shelter for his street people, along with a thrift shop; and finally, providing a shelter complete with a wide range of social services. Like Jesus, Trevor did not ask the poor on the streets to justify their need. He just responded as generously as a young person can. I often think of Trevor when I hear hateful remarks about "welfare queens" or encounter people who are afraid to get involved.

But Jesus' healing miracle also reminds me of the tremendous pain that parents experience when their children die before they do. In my own parish, I remember vividly the experience of a parishioner whose 26-year-old son was killed in a drive-by shooting. Months later, she spoke to the congregation with tears of gratitude for the outpouring of love she experienced from her Church family. Here was the Body of Christ—Jesus today—embracing the grieving mother. So many other mothers and fathers grieve in our society, and around the world, over the death of their children, especially the senseless killing of children by other children.

Other parents experience a similar sense of loss when their children lose themselves to drugs and crime. As a prison volunteer working closely with the Violent Offenders Program (VOP) at one of Missouri's correctional centers, I sense the pain of families and their incarcerated members. Also I have the privilege of witnessing incredible conversions in the lives of some of these inmates. Often they encounter the unconditional love and faithful presence of "outmates" (outside volunteers) who really do bring Jesus into their hearts. After the intense three-day "Residents Encounter Christ" (REC) retreats, and after an equally intense three-month VOP experience, I see these men "arise" to new life. I see family members rejoicing over the "resurrection" of their incarcerated sons, husbands, and brothers. Through the faithful love of Christian outmates, Jesus is able to say to inmates as he did to the son of the widow of Naim, "Young man, I tell you, arise!" (v. 14).

Invitation to Group Sharing

1. Who are the grieving parents and lost young people in my own locale?

2. What are some of the barriers that keep me from being more compassionate and that keep our faith community from becoming more involved in reaching out to those who are lost?

3. What can I, individually, and we, as a faith community, do to remove some of these barriers and be more responsive?

4. What can I do to reach out to one grieving parent or one lost young person in the weeks ahead?

Invitation to Act

Determine a specific action (individual or group) that flows from your sharing. This should be your primary consideration. When choosing an individual action, determine what you will do and share it with the group.

When choosing a group action, determine who will take responsibility for different aspects of the action. The following are secondary suggestions:

1. Read and listen to the accounts of suffering in the newspaper and on the news with an open and prayerful spirit.

2. Prayerfully read books or watch videos on the lives of compassionate Christians like Trevor Farrell (*Trevor's Place;* Harper & Row), Sr. Helen Prejean (*Dead Man Walking;* Random House). Show the video *Dead Man Walking* in your parish. You may also like to contact Sr. Helen Prejean at www.prejean.org.

3. Do an inventory of your skills, experience, and opportunities for service; of the internal and external barriers to your becoming more involved in compassionate service; and of how you spend your time. Make whatever changes you need to in order to make room for compassionate service, at least within your own family and friendship circles.

4. Identify some of the groups in your community working with impoverished single parents, with inmates and their families and victims, and with grieving families (for example, hospice); choose one to meet with to see if your skills and experience can be helpful.

5. As a total faith community, consider reaching out to a prison inmate and offering hospitality and support when he or she is released. Consider Jesus' words about how much more joy there is in heaven about one "lost sheep" who is found than the 99 others. Consult www.ipj-ppj.org for more information on the Institute for Peace and Justice Violent Offender Program (VOP).

Invitation to Closing Prayer

Give thanks to God (aloud or silently) for insights gained, for desires awakened, for directions clarified, for the gift of one another's openness and sensitivity. Conclude with the following (recite aloud together):

Jesus, often we are so busy
that we do not even notice those around us
who are grieving,
those who are dead or lost.

And even when we do notice,
we are often afraid to reach out.

We do not know what to say
or what might be asked of us,
or where we will be led.

Forgive us for our misplaced priorities,
for our selfishness, and for our fear.

Open our eyes and touch our hearts
so that we may respond
with your immediate and compassionate love
to those who are hurting around us.

Lead us into places and lives
where people cry out for your mercy and healing
but are often ignored or punished vindictively.

Help us be the instruments of your mercy
and healing, and heal us in the process.

This we ask in your name,
you who live and reign with God the Father,
in the unity of the Holy Spirit,
now and forever. Amen.

ELEVENTH SUNDAY IN ORDINARY TIME

The Discipleship of Women—
A Gift of Our Church

Invitation to Pray

Pause for a few moments of silence and enter more deeply into the presence of God.

Opening Song
One Bread, One Body

Proclaim the Gospel
Luke 7:36-50
Pardon of the Sinful Woman

Take a few minutes to savor a word, a phrase, a question, or a feeling that rises up in you. Reflect on this quietly or share it aloud.

The other Scripture readings of the day are
2 Samuel 12:7-10, 13,
Psalm 32:1-2, 5, 7, 11,
and Galatians 2:16, 19-21.

Invitation to Reflect on the Gospel

This story of pardon shows two different responses to the ministry of Jesus. Suspecting Jesus is a prophet, the Pharisee invites him to a banquet at his house, but his self-righteousness leads to little love and forgiveness. The sinful woman, however, expresses her faith in actions, which lead to forgiveness. Her expression, with her display of love, gives Jesus the occasion to teach a profound lesson of divine forgiveness and a response of gratitude.

Time and again it is the women around Jesus who extend themselves in service; who stay by his side no matter what the danger or pain; who more readily understand his message of simplicity, service, and sacrifice; and who respond quickly and enthusiastically to his call. Far too often, it is the men around Jesus who flaunt their authority and position and resist his message; who desert him in danger; who are quick to judge and exclude others; who are rigidly bound to the past; and who are slow to understand Jesus' new Way.

Just like the Pharisee in today's Gospel, we acknowledge Jesus as prophet, but often do not see him in our everyday relations. Too many of us, women as well as men, fail to recognize sexism at home, or work, or Church. As Christ's compassionate disciples today, we face the challenge of expressing our love of Jesus in our daily relationships and policies. We need to recognize, we need to acknowledge, we need to change, personally and socially.

We, who recognize this need for change, need to start with ourselves and any lingering sexism we may find in our own attitudes and behaviors. As we make our vocabulary more inclusive, we can encourage inclusive language where we work and worship. As we eliminate sexist put-downs in our own conversation, we can challenge such put-downs in the mouths of others. As we change our own sexist division of tasks and responsibilities and exclusive patterns at home (for example, men watching sports and women preparing meals at every family gathering), we can do the same in our workplace, parish, and other groups and organizations.

Invitation to Group Sharing

1. In what ways or situations am I like some of the Pharisees whose rigid, judgmental, and legalistic thinking and acting Jesus condemned? Are there ways in which our faith community is guilty of this thinking as well?

2. In what ways or situations have I embodied the humble and generous compassion, service, and repentance of the woman Jesus extols?

3. Where do I see sexism first hand? How does my silence in this witness, or my defense of the status quo, fare for those excluded?

4. What steps can I, and we as a faith community, take to become less like some of the Pharisees and more like the sorrowful woman?

Invitation to Act

Determine a specific action (individual or group) that flows from your sharing. This should be your primary consideration. When choosing an individual action, determine what you will do and share it with the group. When choosing a group action, determine who will take responsibility for different aspects of the action. The following are secondary suggestions:

1. Add to your reading list the biographies of compassionate and courageous women—some traditional and some not so traditional saintly women, for example, Catherine of Siena, Teresa of Avila, Mother Elizabeth Seton, Sojourner Truth, or Kateri Tekawitha.

2. Identify sexist patterns and behaviors where you live, work, and/or worship and pick one to focus your prayer and action on first.

3. Offer a gender sensitivity training for your parish staff and parishioners, especially those involved in ministry. Be sure to include young adults and adolescents.

Invitation to Closing Prayer

Give thanks to God (aloud or silently) for insights gained, for desires awakened, for directions clarified, for the gift of one another's openness and sensitivity. Conclude with the following (recite aloud together):

Jesus, your example of praising women and
including them in your ministry
is a challenging one for us today.

Send us your Spirit of inclusive love
to break open our narrow thinking
and our exclusionary behavior.

Help us to be like the woman who anointed your feet.

Above all, let it be our love
that humbly and persistently speaks
to those whose rigidity
continues to wound persons deeply
and wound the Church as well.

Jesus, you spoke hard words
when you said you came to sow division,
not peaceful conformity.

Help us to embrace this hard love and work tirelessly
on behalf of your prophetic words and witness.

We pray, as always, in your name,
Jesus, our Christ and our brother. Amen.

TWELFTH SUNDAY IN ORDINARY TIME

Christian Discipleship Embraces the Cross

Invitation to Pray

Pause for a few moments of silence and enter more deeply into the presence of God.

Opening Song
Lord of the Dance

Proclaim the Gospel

Luke 9:18-24
Jesus and His Family

Take a few minutes to savor a word, a phrase, a question, or a feeling that rises up in you. Reflect on this quietly or share it aloud.

The other Scripture readings of the day are

Zechariah 12:10-11; 13:1,
Psalm 63:2-6, 8-9,
and Galatians 3:26-29.

Invitation to Reflect on the Gospel

Peter was able to proclaim Jesus as "the Messiah of God" (v. 20), but he had little understanding of what this Messiahship entailed. In fact, he was horrified by Jesus' references to his passion and death, meriting one of Jesus' harshest rebukes in Scripture: "Get behind me, Satan!" (Matthew 16:23). Personally, I am more petrified than horrified by these words. Jesus tells us that if we want to be his disciples, we must deny ourselves and take up our cross daily. The key word in this phrase, I have come to realize after many years of trying to live this imperative, is "our"—"take up *our* cross" (cf. v. 23). Yes, we have to follow Jesus to the cross to get to resurrection, but our cross is not the same as Jesus' cross. This realization came most graphically to me on a pilgrimage to Assisi several years ago. I wanted to experience, as much as I could, the lives of Francis and Clare, so I hiked up to the caves where Francis and his early followers often retreated in prayer. I was a little fearful walking into one of those caves. Because Francis so identified with the crucified Jesus, I knew that placing myself near where Francis prayed would mean some kind of encounter with that same crucified One. What I discovered still comforts as well as challenges me.

In the cave was a pair of twigs bound together like a cross. The horizontal twig was longer at one end, so the cross kept tipping over no matter how I tried to stand it up. Then I noticed a notch in the longer section of the horizontal twig. When I broke the piece off, the cross balanced perfectly. Amazingly the small piece I had broken off fit my hand perfectly. Slowly it dawned on me: the cross of Jesus is not complete until I break off and grab hold of my piece. The longer I held that piece in prayerful silence, the more comforted I felt. Yes, I will have to take up the cross of Jesus, accept his yoke on my shoulders, but I will not be overwhelmed. Jesus will never let that cross be more than I can bear.

Similarly, each time I receive the blood of Jesus in Communion, I am aware of Jesus' question, "Can you drink the cup that I am going to drink" (Matthew 20:22)? I have found that I can say "yes" when I realize it is not the same cup Jesus asks me to embrace. Henri Nouwen's beautiful reflection on "the cup of Jesus" has helped me a lot. Each of us has our own particular "cup" to embrace. Each day I am asked to pick up my unique cup and drink it to the full. Where is the grace to do this? Among other graces, Jesus has given us his own eucharistic presence to inspire and sustain us.

Invitation to Group Sharing

1. What situations, persons, and/or areas of my life seem like crosses that Jesus wants me to carry as his disciple?

2. What keeps me from embracing these crosses more generously?

3. What supports or graces are available to help me with my crosses? How can I allow the Eucharist to sustain my daily crosses better?

4. What can I do individually, and our faith community do corporately, to encourage and support one another in embracing our crosses with the wholehearted love of Jesus?

Invitation to Act

Determine a specific action (individual or group) that flows from your sharing. This should be your primary consideration. When choosing an individual action, determine what you will do and share it with the group. When choosing a group action, determine who will take responsibility for different aspects of the action. The following are secondary suggestions:

1. Find crucifixes that have particular meaning for you and place one in your prayer site at home. If possible, place one at your desk at work or elsewhere in your daily environment. Each morning as you dress, put a crucifix around your neck or elsewhere on your person—each time with a prayer and a kiss—as a more intimate reminder to live that day in the spirit of the crucified Jesus.

2. Consider designating one day a week as a "solidarity day" when you pray, fast in some way, and do a

sacrificial action on behalf of some person or group that is suffering greatly.

3. Take a difficult but necessary part of your life (for example, parenting a teenager, caring for a disagreeable family member, dealing with a difficult co-worker or neighbor) and reframe it, with the help of a spouse, close friend, and/or spiritual director, as a unique opportunity to learn and live the sacrificial love of Jesus.

Invitation to Closing Prayer

Give thanks to God (aloud or silently) for insights gained, for desires awakened, for directions clarified, for the gift of one another's openness and sensitivity. Conclude with the following (recite aloud together):

Jesus, how often we find ourselves like Peter—quick to call you our Lord and Savior, but slow to embrace your sacrificial and saving "Way."

We confess we are more comfortable with your Resurrection than we are with your passion. Thank you, Jesus, for your example of sacrificial love. Thank you for your loving assurance that our yokes will, indeed, be easy and our burdens light (see Matthew 11:30).

Help us to see our daily struggles as opportunities to follow you by embracing our cross and drinking our cup as wholeheartedly as you did.

Help us to find "soul" brothers and sisters willing to embrace this sacrificial calling with us.

And whenever we cry out in our pain for mercy, please send us the same consoling Spirit who consoled you in your moment of agony in the Garden of Gethsemane.

We pray in your name, Jesus, to our heavenly Father, with whom you live and reign, in the unity of the Holy Spirit, one God, forever and ever. Amen.

THIRTEENTH SUNDAY IN ORDINARY TIME

Here I Am, Lord

Invitation to Pray

Pause for a few moments of silence and enter more deeply into the presence of God.

Opening Song

Here I Am, Lord
or
We are Called

Proclaim the Gospel

Luke 9:51-62
Samaritan Inhospitality

Take a few minutes to savor a word, a phrase, a question, or a feeling that rises up in you. Reflect on this quietly or share it aloud.

The other Scripture readings of the day are

1 Kings 19:16b, 19-21,
Psalm 16:1-2, 5, 7-11,
and Galatians 5:1, 13-18.

Invitation to Reflect on the Gospel

When we are young and idealistic, we often find ourselves able to say with genuine enthusiasm, "I'll go with you anywhere, Lord! Here I am, Lord; send me." The first apostles dropped their nets and responded immediately to Jesus' invitation to "follow me" (v. 59). They swelled with pride as the crowds swelled in size, especially when Jesus climbed on the donkey and made his entry into Jerusalem on that first Palm Sunday.

The first apostles thought their kingly Messiah was riding in triumph to claim his earthly throne. Even when Jesus chose a lowly donkey rather than the regal horse as his steed, they still did not understand that he was going into his final deadly confrontation with the forces of domination and exploitation within the Roman and Jewish communities. But it did not take long for the glory of Palm Sunday to become the terror of Good Friday. His followers scattered in fear. Peter, his chosen representative, denied his master three times. They clearly could not keep their promise to follow him wherever he would go.

Jesus' sobering words to Peter should be sobering to us as well, someone will "lead you where you do not want to go" (John 21:18). The enthusiastic early promises we make are purified through suffering. Like Jesus and Peter, God will lead us where we would rather not go. In the Garden of Gethsemane, Jesus pleaded in terror, "let this cup pass from me ..." (Matthew 26:39). But Jesus was quickly consoled by God's Spirit of Love, so that he could yield himself completely to his Father's will, "not as I will, but as you will" (Matthew 26:39). Realizing that Jesus knows full well the fearful reality of embracing the call to sacrificial love, we can pray in confidence for the grace to follow him to the cross, and through the cross to Easter and the fullness of life.

If Abraham and Sarah in their old age could pick up and leave their ancestral land in faith and go wherever God would lead them, perhaps we can approach the unknowns in our own journeys with the same courageous faith. If the fearful Peter, who denied his master three times, could be brought by the power of the Holy Spirit to embrace death by crucifixion, perhaps we can endure those lesser forms of persecution that we may experience when we say our "yes."

Invitation to Group Sharing

1. Are there places or situations that I am resisting at this time in my life, when, in fact, it may be God who is prompting me to go there?

2. How might I respond better when God leads me where I would rather not go?

3. What can I do to find the help I need in order to go more courageously into these difficult situations as an emissary of God's love?

4. What can we do as a faith community to nurture this sense of mission and openness to the will of God in our worship, educational programs, and outreach ministries?

Invitation to Act

Determine a specific action (individual or group) that flows from your sharing. This should be your primary consideration. When choosing an individual action, determine what you will do and share it with the group. When choosing a group action, determine who will take responsibility for different aspects of the action. The following are secondary suggestions:

1. Set aside time this year for a mini-retreat in which the focus is on where God is leading you on your spiritual journey. This could be done individually, with the person you are closest to, or with a small prayer group, or ministry group.

2. Each time you are in a difficult situation, make sure you allow ample time to reflect prayerfully and listen. Meditate on the lives of the heroes of faith—from the list in Chapters 10 and 11 of the Letter to the Hebrews, to the contemporary heroes of faith identified in earlier sessions.

3. Find or form a group of believers who want to be more compassionate and courageous in standing with the victims of injustice. The support and accountability that a group provides is an essential ingredient in prophetic ministry.

Invitation to Closing Prayer

Give thanks to God (aloud or silently) for insights gained, for desires awakened, for directions clarified, for the gift of one another's openness and sensitivity.

Conclude with the following, which is a paraphrase of the prophetic reluctance, but eventual submission, we find in Jeremiah 1 and Isaiah 7.

Jeremiah cited his youth, as well as fear, as his excuses (Jeremiah 1:6). While most of us cannot use youth as our excuse, we are quick to cite our lack of experience or training. And none of us easily chooses what we anticipate will be a fearful and painful experience.

Have one person be the narrator, one read the words of God, and the rest of the group read the responses of the reluctant prophet.

And the Lord said,
"Go!"

and I said, "Who, me?"

And God said,
"Yes, you!"

**And I said, "But I'm not ready yet,
and there is company coming,**

**and I can't leave my kids;
you know there's no one to take my place."**

And God said,
"You're stalling."

Again God said,
"Go!"

and I said, "But I don't want to."

And God said,
"I didn't ask if you wanted to."

**And I said, "Listen, I'm not the kind of person
to get involved in controversy.
Besides, my family won't like it,
and what will other parishioners
and neighbors think!"**

And God said,
"Why do you care?"

And yet a third time God said,
"Go!"

And I said, "Do I have to?"

And God said,
"Do you love me?"

**And I said, "Look, I'm scared...
People are going to hate me and
cut me up into little pieces.
I can't take it all by myself."**

And God said,
"Where do you think I'll be?"

And God said,
"Go!"

And I sighed, "Here I am; send me."

(Adapted from a prayer by Lois Hodrick,
Maryknoll Magazine, November 1984.)

Fourteenth Sunday in Ordinary Time

The Reign of God Is at Hand and in Our Hearts

Invitation to Pray

Pause for a few moments of silence and enter more deeply into the presence of God.

Song

This Little Light of Mine
or They'll Know We Are Christians

Proclaim the Gospel

Luke 10:1-9
Mission of the Seventy-Two

Take a few minutes to savor a word, a phrase, a question, or a feeling that rises up in you. Reflect on this quietly or share it aloud.

The other Scripture readings of the day are

Isaiah 66:10-14c,
Psalm 66:1-7, 16, 20,
and Galatians 6:14-18.

Invitation to Reflect on the Gospel

When we go into situations of ministry as careful listeners, we discover that the first and perhaps the best thing we can give people is our loving attentiveness. Inviting nursing home residents, as well as older people in other living situations, to share some of their life story is tremendously affirming. Ministry becomes mutual service when we engage people with loving attentiveness.

Our hands can be instruments of loving service every bit as much as our ears. We do not have to become masseurs or masseuses to learn how to love others with our hands, although massage can be a very tangible and immediate way of communicating God's love. Loving touch is a powerful purveyor of God's love. I will never forget the lesson I learned years ago from a bunch of children living at a shelter in downtown St. Louis. I would show up monthly as a clown with a bag of Hershey Kisses. But instead of grabbing at the Kisses when they raced up to me, they went straight for the large red heart on my costume. They knew that whenever they pressed my heart, I would give them a big hug. They would rather have human hugs than chocolate Kisses. The reign of God is at hand. It is as close as our own loving hands.

But bringing loving eyes and open hearts into our many daily encounters can also make us vulnerable. We may be misunderstood, ignored, or sometimes put down. But Jesus asks us to be willing to be a "lamb" as he was—a sacrificial lover in the midst of a "wolfish" society. If we imitate the vulnerable love of Jesus, we become instruments of his transformation of the world. Through us as through Jesus, the reign of God is at hand. I remember so clearly the story about a soldier in Italy in World War II who found a statue of Jesus that was missing its hands. At the base of the statue were written the words, "I have no hands but yours." The reign of God is truly in our hands.

Invitation to Group Sharing

1. What can I do to become more present, attentive, and affirming to those around me? Be specific.

2. What aspects or situations of my life could be seen as areas of ministry where Jesus wants me to go as the emissary of his love and peace?

3. What keeps me from being more explicit and bold about proclaiming in word and deed God's love and peace in these situations of ministry?

Invitation to Act

Determine a specific action (individual or group) that flows from your sharing. This should be your primary consideration. When choosing an individual action, determine what you will do and share it with the group. When choosing a group action, determine who will take responsibility for different aspects of the action. The following are secondary suggestions:

1. Kneel, if possible, at the end of your morning prayer and ask Jesus to send you into your world each day as an emissary of his love and peace.

2. Discover more about Francis of Assisi's "*Pace e bene*" ("peace and good") greeting to people he met each day and follow Francis' example of loving people with his eyes.

3. As a way of implementing Jesus' directive to his disciples to go forth in pairs, find a partner or small group to go with into your situations of ministry, whenever it is appropriate.

Invitation to Closing Prayer

Give thanks to God (aloud or silently) for insights gained, for desires awakened, for directions clarified, for the gift of one another's openness and sensitivity. Conclude with the following (recite aloud together):

Our Father in heaven,
hallowed be your name,

your kingdom come,
your will be done,
on earth as in heaven. (Matthew 6:9-10)

Yes, may your kingdom come more fully on earth
through Jesus, your chosen one,
and those others that Jesus chooses
in every generation.

Jesus, we did not choose you;
rather, you chose us
—to go forth as emissaries of God's love and peace
into every part and place of our lives.

What an awesome calling
—to be your eyes, your ears, your hands for others.

Free us from the selfishness
and fears that hold us back.

Still us at the beginning of each day,
so that we may hear your voice
and feel your love blessing us and sending us forth.

Open us to the giftedness of those with whom we
    minister,
and help us become more attentive and supportive
    allies.

All of these blessings we ask in your name,
as you told us to,
you who live and reign
with the Father and the Holy Spirit,
one God, forever and ever. Amen.

FIFTEENTH SUNDAY IN ORDINARY TIME

What Does It Mean to Be a Good Neighbor?

Invitation to Pray

Pause for a few moments of silence and enter more deeply into the presence of God.

Opening Song
Be Not Afraid

Proclaim the Gospel

Luke 10:25-37
The Greatest Commandment

Take a few minutes to savor a word, a phrase, a question, or a feeling that rises up in you. Reflect on this quietly or share it aloud.

The other Scripture readings of the day are

Deuteronomy 30:10-14,
Psalm 69:14, 17, 30-31, 33-34, 36-37,
or Psalm 19:8, 9, 10, 11,
and Colossians 1:15-20.

Invitation to Reflect on the Gospel

In the parable of the good Samaritan, Jesus challenges us in at least three ways: how close we should get to suffering, how generously we should respond, and how inclusive our compassion should be.

First, notice what the priest and Levite did. They crossed the road so that they would not have to get too close to the injured man who seemed to be dead. Touching a dead body would render them unsuitable for service of God. Perhaps they did not want to see.

Could it be that the wealthy in desperately poor lands sometimes ride in cars with shades drawn so they do not have to see the beggars surrounding them? What a contrast with the example of Mary as she stood beneath the cross and embraced all the pain that a mother can embrace when her child is tortured and killed before her eyes! Mary and the good Samaritan challenge us to move toward suffering rather than away from it. When we engage life "up close and personal," with open eyes and an open heart, we are much more likely to be moved to compassionate action.

The second challenge the good Samaritan poses for us is how generous our compassionate action should be. Jesus raises the standard on what it means to be "good." In many situations, it is not enough to make donations of cash, food, or clothes; send a sympathy card; or promise to pray for others. Notice the extent of the service provided by the good Samaritan. He personally comforted the injured man, transported him to a safe haven, paid for his care, and promised to return to see if more help was needed. He may have arrived late at his original destination, but sometimes God has other destinations in mind for us when we set out at the beginning of each day.

Thirdly, Jesus uses the good Samaritan to underline his constant teaching that the test of Christian love is not how much we love those who love us, but how much we love those who do not love us. Jesus' disciples are to imitate their master's inclusive embrace of all people and the example of the good Samaritan. We are called to extend our compassion to our "enemies": those who get on our nerves, those who sometimes put us down, those who cannot repay us, those who often disagree with us, as well as those who seek to hurt us.

What a witness people like Bud Welch are in forgiving those who kill their loved ones! Deeply hurt by the killing of his daughter in the Oklahoma City bombing in 1995, Bud reached out to the perpetrator, Timothy McVeigh, and his family. What a witness a group of African American youth provided when they went into white, south St. Louis County to help residents sandbag their homes against the flooding Mississippi River in 1993! People who cross racial, religious, and ethnic barriers to help others are often criticized by both sides. But it takes just this kind of inclusive compassion to break down these barriers to the full realization of God's beloved community.

Invitation to Group Sharing

1. Who can I help better in my life?

2. How can I respond with compassion?

3. In doing so, how can I deliberately move beyond my comfort zone?

Invitation to Act

Determine a specific action (individual or group) that flows from your sharing. This should be your primary consideration. When choosing an individual action, determine what you will do and share it with the group. When choosing a group action, determine who will take responsibility for different aspects of the action. The following are secondary suggestions:

1. Pray the Sorrowful Mysteries of the rosary.

2. Test your comfort zone regularly. Reach out, at least once each day, even if only with a smile or greeting, to those who are different from you or those who do not especially like you.

3. Find one person or group of persons that many people despise and begin associating with them. Explore how you might be able to be of service to them and stand with them privately and publicly when they need "outside" allies.

4. Encourage your faith community to invite some of "the least" of Jesus' people to become members. Include in your prayer ministry and your outreach programs those who are imprisoned; those suffering from AIDS; those who are economically poor or newly-arrived immigrants; and innocent victims of war, like the children of Iraq.

Invitation to Closing Prayer

Give thanks to God (aloud or silently) for insights gained, for desires awakened, for directions clarified, for the gift of one another's openness and sensitivity. Conclude with the following (recite aloud together):

Mary, you stood at the foot of the cross
and ached with the suffering
your only Child was enduring.

Please help us open our eyes and hearts and hands
to those children of God
suffering in our midst.

Thank you for nurturing
a compassionate heart in your Son, Jesus,
and help us nurture compassionate hearts
in the children in our lives.

Jesus, help us stand with people,
as you did, when they are victimized
or vilified because of their sexual orientation,
their race or nationality, a disease they have,
or criminal deeds they have done.

Help us, O gracious God,
become "good neighbors" to all your children.

Help us to become brothers and sisters,
in deeds as well as in words,
and advance the coming of your beloved community.

We pray in the name of your Son, Jesus,
who lives and reigns with you and the Holy Spirit,
one God, forever and ever. Amen.

SIXTEENTH SUNDAY IN ORDINARY TIME

Listening to Jesus

Invitation to Pray

Pause for a few moments of silence and enter more deeply into the presence of God.

Opening Song
You Are Near

Proclaim the Gospel

Luke 10:38-42
Martha and Mary

Take a few minutes to savor a word, a phrase, a question, or a feeling that rises up in you. Reflect on this quietly or share it aloud.

The other Scripture readings of the day are

Genesis 18:1-10a,
Psalm 15:2-5,
and Colossians 1:24-28.

Invitation to Reflect on the Gospel

It would appear that Jesus is castigating Martha for her acts of hospitality and praising Mary for the better portion she had chosen. The Martha in us screams, "unfair!" What is going on in this very familiar story from Luke's Gospel?

It is unlikely that Jesus was devaluing the very important biblical principle of hospitality. Hospitality was a sacred act and a crucial responsibility for every believer. Divine hospitality was a metaphor used to describe God's protection and care. To offer hospitality to another was synonymous with offering it to God.

In the fifteenth chapter of John's Gospel, Jesus challenged his listeners to action; yet in today's Gospel, he endorsed Mary's posture of contemplation. One cannot deny that Jesus upheld action as an important value. It nevertheless appears today as if Mary's stance of "being"/contemplation is regarded as a higher value. So which is it, really?

First century listeners would have been shocked at the suggestion that hospitality should take a back seat. It was, after all, a sign and symbol of God's presence and action. A sign of one's right relationship with God was evidenced by loving action. Jesus was not making a comparison of spiritual values; he was inviting deep transformation of the whole person.

In John's fifteenth chapter, Jesus insisted that his audience's response to God be rooted in concrete action. And in today's Gospel, Jesus challenged Martha's orientation toward "doing" and praised Mary's posture of "being." Jesus was inviting disciples (men and women) to step out of their expected norm, to look at things from a new perspective, and encounter the God of surprise. Whenever disciples stretch themselves, move into uncharted waters, and listen to God anew, they invite the transformation of every area of life. Those who are naturally drawn to a ministry of service need to spend time in prayer and contemplation, and those who are drawn to contemplation need to ground their prayer in action. One feeds the other.

Today's Gospel reminds us that the greatest action one can perform is to love the Lord with one's entire being. Jesus invites us to step outside the routine of our lives, even the admirable routine, and abide with him. Our service will not last if not rooted in the contemplation of God's Word.

Invitation to Group Sharing

1. Who are some people I have known whose primary disposition is that of "doing" or of "being"? What have I learned from them?

2. Which of the "doing" or "being" aspects of my life needs to be stronger? Explain.

3. How would I respond if someone invited me to step out of my norm and take a risk? What would it cost me?

4. How does today's Gospel invite us to grow in our relationship with God? How can we, as a group, help one another become transformed by today's Gospel?

Invitation to Act

Determine a specific action (individual or group) that flows from your sharing. This should be your primary consideration. When choosing an individual action, determine what you will do and share it with the group. When choosing a group action, determine who will take responsibility for different aspects of the action. The following are secondary suggestions:

1. Those who determined that their primary orientation was that of "being" might choose one or two acts of service or hospitality this week, such as visiting a nursing home, serving a meal at a soup kitchen, or helping a neighbor. This experience of service might then be brought into your prayer and reflection. What did God teach you from the experience?

2. Those who determined that their primary orientation was that of "doing" might take two evenings to sit quietly for half an hour with the first

or second reading from the coming Sunday's liturgy and simply allow it to speak to the quiet recesses of their soul. Reflect on the way in which the readings speak to your experiences of service and hospitality.

3. Set aside at least five minutes each day to pray for those who wish to challenge themselves accordingly.

Invitation to Closing Prayer

Give thanks to God (aloud or silently) for insights gained, for desires awakened, for directions clarified, for the gift of one another's openness and sensitivity. Conclude with the following:

Lord God,
in your wisdom you invite us
out of our complacency.

You open our eyes
to see you with new vision.

You open our hearts
to love you with greater passion,
and you open our hands to serve you
with the purest intentions.

Lead us more deeply
into the mystery of discipleship
so that we may follow you
with steadfast faithfulness.

Give us the heart of Mary,
so we can be transformed by your Word
and fortified by your presence.

Give us the mind of Martha,
so we can diligently accomplish your mission,
But above all, continue to invite us
into intimate and
lasting relationship.

We ask this through Christ our Lord. Amen.

SEVENTEENTH SUNDAY IN ORDINARY TIME

God's Incredible Generosity

Invitation to Pray

Pause for a few moments of silence and enter more deeply into the presence of God.

Opening Song
Come, Holy Ghost

Proclaim the Gospel
Luke 11:1-13
The Lord's Prayer

Take a few minutes to savor a word, a phrase, a question, or a feeling that rises up in you. Reflect on this quietly or share it aloud.

The other Scripture readings of the day are
Genesis 18:20-32,
Psalm 138:1-8,
and Colossians 2:12-14.

Invitation to Reflect on the Gospel

In first century Palestine, groups were recognized by the way they prayed, so when the disciples asked Jesus how to pray they were asking him to give them an identity. Christian identity is rooted in the community's prayer.

In today's Gospel, Jesus presents us with his catechism on prayer. Jesus' prayer was presented to the community, not to individuals. The Bible presents us with two forms of the Lord's Prayer—Matthew's and

Luke's. Matthew's version (Matthew 6:9-13) is future-oriented, whereas the version we read today from Luke is present-centered (with an eye to the future). The petition for daily bread is a request that God provide the physical necessities needed to carry out his mission on earth. Jesus' prayer asks that disciples not be entrapped by the daily seductions of life and that they never stop praying.

Jesus uses a parable to illustrate God's incredible generosity. He introduces us to the person who unabashedly and persistently knocks on the door of a reluctant neighbor. His point? If this reluctant neighbor eventually answers the door, how much more will God show his love to those who also come knocking? How will God answer? God will give good gifts. What are the good gifts God will give? The Holy Spirit. Jesus invites us to pray for the gift of God's Spirit. The Holy Spirit will gift us with everything we need to proclaim the Good News, and invite others to experience the reign of God in the here and now as we await the future kingdom.

Jesus wants us to be bold—to have a little spunk. He invites us to pray that God gives us our future hope, but that it be given to us right now. We are not to take "no" for an answer! Prayer is not for the timid; conscientious persistence gets results.

The *Roman Missal* reminds us that the Lord's Prayer proclaimed in the liturgy is a request for daily food and for the forgiveness of sins, so that the Eucharist which is holy, may be given to us who are also holy. We, who are holy, are strengthened and nourished by the power of the Spirit to go out and proclaim the reign of God. For this we pray; for this we lay down our lives. The prayer Jesus taught us is rooted in love and concern for others. Are we ready to go forth boldly? Are we willing?

Invitation to Group Sharing

1. Has my praying the Lord's Prayer become too routine? How might I offer this beautiful prayer with greater devotion and expectancy?

2. What does this Gospel say to me about my own prayer life? How do I feel about the Gospel's insistence that persistence pays off?

3. Have I been the reluctant neighbor when someone "knocked" on my door? What were my feelings or actions afterward? How can I turn a reluctant attitude to one of generosity?

Invitation to Act

Determine a specific action (individual or group) that flows from your sharing. This should be your primary consideration. When choosing an individual action, determine what you will do and share it with the group. When choosing a group action, determine who will take responsibility for different aspects of the action. The following are secondary suggestions:

1. Each day this week take a phrase from the Lord's Prayer and reflect upon it. At the end of the week, pray the entire prayer, and see if there are any new insights from your week-long meditation.

2. Since this Gospel is directly related to mission, try to apply the principles each day in your marketplace experience; for example, pray without stopping, pray for the Spirit, pray persistently. Perhaps you might center your prayer for the needs of one other person this week, that is, a family member, a co-worker, etc. Carry his or her name on an index card. Keep it in your pocket, wallet, or purse as a reminder.

3. Return to praying for a petition you may have given up on.

4. Perhaps every member of the group might commit to talking to one other person about his or her relationship with Christ this week and report back to the group.

Invitation to Closing Prayer

Give thanks to God (aloud or silently) for insights gained, for desires awakened, for directions clarified, for the gift of one another's openness and sensitivity. Conclude with the following:

God of power and might,
you teach us the marvels of the universe.

You have given us your Son,
the revelation of your divine presence, and
you invite us into deep and everlasting relationship.

Help us to grow in our desire to know you:
our hunger to be fed with your love
and our longing to be imbued
with the wisdom of your Spirit.

Strengthen us to become effective witnesses of the
   Gospel
and to promote the reign of God in the world.

We ask this through Christ our Lord. Amen.

Conclude with The Lord's Prayer.

EIGHTEENTH SUNDAY IN ORDINARY TIME

Where Is Security?

Invitation to Pray

Pause for a few moments of silence and enter more deeply into the presence of God.

Song

The Lord Hears the Cry of the Poor

Proclaim the Gospel

Luke 12:13-21
Parable of the Rich Fool

Take a few minutes to savor a word, a phrase, a question, or a feeling that rises up in you. Reflect on this quietly or share it aloud.

The other Scripture readings of the day are

Ecclesiastes 1:2; 2:21-23,
Psalm 90:3-6, 12-14, 17,
and Colossians 3:1-5, 9-11.

Invitation to Reflect on the Gospel

A sobering moment is interrupted by what appears to be a trite exchange. Jesus and his disciples are on the road to Jerusalem. They have been discussing the serious implications of the road ahead. Jesus is asked to settle a rather mundane issue regarding inheritance. Luke uses this vignette as a teachable moment on the seductive power of material possessions. Excessive concentration on material goods is human nature's way of dealing with the ambiguities of life and its fleeting nature. The rich man in Jesus' parable believed that his overly abundant crops would buy his future security. In the end they provided nothing. His security was misplaced.

Material possessions do not offer security. Our security rests in God alone. We are to spend our lives promoting the reign of God on earth as we await the reign of God to come. Life is our greatest gift. The challenge of the Gospel is to put our energy and our trust in things that do not perish, and place our security in God, the lavish giver of all gifts.

Christians are invited to let go of their attachment to material possessions. The disciples were not only invited to let go of the fear of their futures and to divest themselves of their attachments, but also to turn their lives over completely to the Master of their destiny. Only then would they know true freedom as God's children. The amassing of wealth for a future day is not a response of faith according to Luke.

Today's Gospel asks us the difficult question: "Have we been more evangelized by the Gospel of rugged individualism than we have been by the Gospel of Jesus Christ?" A response in faith to the living God who provides and cares for his people is to lay down our lives for one another and to be generous in sharing our wealth with those in need. Spiritual freedom allows Christians to share what they have with others, especially those who hold a special place of honor in Jesus' heart—those who are poor, oppressed, and marginalized.

Invitation to Group Sharing

1. What are some ways our society is seduced by material possessions? What are the symptoms of such seduction?

2. Have I ever been seduced by material goods? How does the story of the rich man speak of my life or my experience? What (if any) are the attachments in my life?

3. Is God the center of my life and the Master of my destiny?

4. What are the inherent challenges of today's Gospel for the community and for me personally?

Invitation to Act

Determine a specific action (individual or group) that flows from your sharing. This should be your primary consideration. When choosing an individual action, determine what you will do and share it with the group. When choosing a group action, determine who will take responsibility for different aspects of the action. The following are secondary suggestions:

1. Spend at least ten minutes a night in prayer and reflection to determine where the areas of excessive attachment to material goods exists in your life, and to pray that the obstacles to your relationship with God be removed. Take action to rectify this.

2. Do those who are poor enter into your discussions about the way in which your money is managed? Are there provisions in your portfolios for those who are poor? Are there any projects at your parish or wider community that support the needs of those who are poor? Perhaps your group might be willing to initiate or participate in such a project.

3. Determine the ways in which your life is overly materialistic and take one small step each week to change. For example, do you have ten sweaters when you only need two or three? Are there clothes and goods around your home that need to be sorted and given to those who are in need?

4. Enter into relationship with one person or family in your community who is poor. Befriend them, as Jesus did. Resolve to not "do" for them, but concentrate on "being" with them.

Invitation to Closing Prayer

Give thanks to God (aloud or silently) for insights gained, for desires awakened, for directions clarified, for the gift of one another's openness and sensitivity. Conclude with the following:

God of Life,
all things are of your making.

You provide us with every good gift.

You bless us with the abundance of the earth
and you ask us to be stewards of that abundance.

Help us to put you first in our lives.

Teach us that all we have comes from you.

Give us the strength
to resist the seductions of this world,
and gift us with your compassion,
so that we may share your gifts
with all the children of the earth.

We ask this through Christ our Lord. Amen.

NINETEENTH SUNDAY IN ORDINARY TIME

Vigilant Disciple

Invitation to Pray

Pause for a few moments of silence and enter more deeply into the presence of God.

Song

Sing with All the Saints in Glory

Proclaim the Gospel

Luke 12:35-40

Vigilant and Faithful Servants

Take a few minutes to savor a word, a phrase, a question, or a feeling that rises up in you. Reflect on this quietly or share it aloud.

The other Scripture readings of the day are

Wisdom 18:6-9,
Psalm 33:1, 12, 18-22,
and Hebrews 11:1-2, 8-19.

Invitation to Reflect on the Gospel

The discussion between Jesus and his disciples is picking up momentum. The stakes are higher. Jesus warns his disciples about what to expect. They will be persecuted because of him. They will encounter hypocrisy. They must rely on God to sustain them. The parable in today's Gospel deals with Jesus' return after his ascension into glory. Jesus is the master who returns after the wedding feast. The parable is an exhortation to vigilance. Luke insists that detachment from worldly goods constitutes preparation for Jesus' second coming.

When the Lord returns, he will serve his guests as they recline at the table. Even after Jesus' glorification, he will return to assume the role of humble servant. Leaders of the community are to follow his example.

Luke presents one of his favorite themes. Disciples are to sell what they have and give to those who are poor. It is the heart of radical discipleship. Jesus acted as the example. Jesus lived the simple life, and in so doing lived in freedom. Such freedom empowers the servant to live for others.

The reference to burning lamps is an allusion to Passover. This reminds the disciples that Christ is the new Passover, and that Christians are heirs to the liberation Jesus won by his death and Resurrection. Jesus invites us to participate in his death and Resurrection (Paschal Mystery) and thus share in his act of redemption. When we offer our suffering to God for the sins of the world, we share in the mystery of the cross.

The allusion to reclining at table is also a reminder of the Eucharist. We remember that Jesus gave us his presence in the midst of his absence. We remember and make present the reality that Jesus died and rose again for us. We memorialize and participate in that event at every celebration of Eucharist. Christians are fed the bread of life so they can, in turn, go out and feed others as they await Jesus' return. Today's Gospel is also a catechism on preparedness. Christians are to be ready for the Master's return at a moment's notice.

Invitation to Group Sharing

1. What does it mean to be prepared? How might that be relevant for Christians today?

2. How do I feel about Jesus' exhortation to sell my possessions and give to those who are poor?

3. Have I ever had the experience of suffering for the sake of another person, or offering my trials and struggles for someone else? If not, would I be willing? Do I see any positive value in such an action?

Invitation to Act

Determine a specific action (individual or group) that flows from your sharing. This should be your primary consideration. When choosing an individual action, determine what you will do and share it with the group. When choosing a group action, determine who will take responsibility for different aspects of the action. The following are secondary suggestions:

1. You might consciously offer the struggles of each day this week for the needs of another.

2. If you were charged with being prepared for the Lord's return, would there be enough evidence to convict you? Make a list of all the things you would like to do to prepare for the second coming of Christ that you are not presently doing. Pray for the strength to become more prepared.

3. This week the group might make a conscious effort to be present to a family in the parish who has just experienced the loss of a loved one. You might all attend the funeral, prepare food, visit family members in their homes, commit to walk with them through their grief, or promise to pray for them.

Invitation to Closing Prayer

Give thanks to God (aloud or silently) for insights gained, for desires awakened, for directions clarified, for the gift of one another's openness and sensitivity. Conclude with the following:

Compassionate God,
you adorn the earth with beauty,
and gift the world with abundant life.

You created human beings in your image
and you instill in them your mercy and compassion.

Strengthen your servants
to grow more fully in the divinity
you have shared with us,
so that we may offer your divine compassion
to those who are broken
by the losses and disappointments of life.

Instill in us the strength and the wisdom
to be prepared for your coming in our lives.

We ask this through Christ our Lord. Amen.

TWENTIETH SUNDAY IN ORDINARY TIME

Baptism by Fire

Invitation to Pray

Pause for a few moments of silence and enter more deeply into the presence of God.

Song

How Can I Keep From Singing

Proclaim the Gospel

Luke 12:49-53

Jesus, a Cause of Division

Take a few minutes to savor a word, a phrase, a question, or a feeling that rises up in you. Reflect on this quietly or share it aloud.

The other Scripture readings of the day are

Jeremiah 38:4-6, 8-10,
Psalm 40:2-4, 18,
and Hebrews 12:1-4.

Invitation to Reflect on the Gospel

Jesus continues to give his disciples their final instructions. Discipleship was proving to be a stormy affair. Conflict was reaching even into families. Christians had to be fortified, and still need to be fortified, to remain strong and to assert their priorities.

Jesus used the imagery of baptism by fire to describe his mission. Baptism by fire was perhaps a reference to the coming of the Spirit at Pentecost, or the judgment at the end of the world. Regardless, Jesus' point is not to be missed, "Listen, folks, there is an urgent message here!"

The peace Jesus came to bring is not peace as we usually understand it. It is discomforting to think that Jesus' message might cause discord in our families. Since we know that God will not tamper with human freedom, people will choose either to follow or not to follow Christ.

Fire has many layers of meaning. It has been used as a metaphor for God's protection. It is a symbol of God's anger, judgment, testing, and purification. Fire was the means God used to reveal himself to Moses. Fire is the energy of God in the midst of Jesus' mission which will purify the earth.

Jesus' baptism by fire is a reference to the horrible ordeal he is about to endure. Only through his purifying trial—torture, humiliation, passion, and death—will the Spirit's tongues of fire be released on the earth. We, too, are invited to embrace our own baptism by fire.

Something so radical automatically invites discord and controversy. In the midst of this purifying fire, families must stand before God and choose. There was an ancient apocalyptic belief that, in the final days, moral depravity would cause families to crumble, to be divided one against the other. Since Jesus inaugurated the final age, this disunity in families was, and is, another sign that the messianic age had arrived. Families today need not be surprised when conflict erupts. They are to remain steadfast and rely on the strength of the Spirit to withstand the test.

Invitation to Group Sharing

1. Do we see a reflection in families today of the discord mentioned in the Gospel? What are the causes?

2. Have I ever experienced discord in my family situation because of Jesus or Gospel values? What did I learn from the experience?

3. How can I create greater unity in my family, especially around faith issues?

4. What does baptism by fire mean to me? Have I ever experienced it? How does this Gospel invite transformation in my life?

Invitation to Act

Determine a specific action (individual or group) that flows from your sharing. This should be your primary consideration. When choosing an individual action, determine what you will do and share it with the group. When choosing a group action, determine who will take responsibility for different aspects of the action. The following are secondary suggestions:

1. Have a family meeting and discuss the implications of this Gospel in your family setting. Continue to hold family meetings weekly or monthly to pray together and share significant happenings.

2. Reach out to someone in your parish, your wider community, or on the national level who is going through a baptism by fire. Offer your prayers and support.

3. As a group reach out to families in distress and offer prayers and support. Volunteer at an abuse center, parents' support groups, or any structures your parish might have to support family life.

Invitation to Closing Prayer

Give thanks to God (aloud or silently) for insights gained, for desires awakened, for directions clarified, for the gift of one another's openness and sensitivity. Conclude with the following:

God of radiant light,
you spoke to Moses through the burning bush.

You led the people through the desert by a pillar of fire.

And you sent the purifying fire of your Spirit
to renew and transform the earth.

Strengthen our families
as we face the seductions of this world.

In these days of fulfillment, purify us
so that when the test comes,
families will stand united in their choice of you.

And in our own baptism by fire,
give us the grace to withstand the trials of our lives,
so that, like gold fashioned by fire,
we, too, may be fashioned in your brilliant image.

We ask this through Christ our Lord. Amen.

TWENTY-FIRST SUNDAY IN ORDINARY TIME

Open the Door

Invitation to Pray

Pause for a few moments of silence and enter more deeply into the presence of God.

Song

Here I Am
or
All Are Welcome

Proclaim the Gospel

Luke 13:22-30
The Narrow Door

Take a few minutes to savor a word, a phrase, a question, or a feeling that rises up in you. Reflect on this quietly or share it aloud.

The other Scripture readings of the day are

Isaiah 66:18-21,
Psalm 117:1-2,
and Hebrews 12:5-7, 11-13.

Invitation to Reflect on the Gospel

A curtain veils today's Gospel. It is the realization that Jesus is on the way to Jerusalem. Things have become quite serious. Jesus is nearing the end of his earthly mission. History stands on the threshold of salvation. Jerusalem holds its breath as it awaits the somber event to come. The entire Gospel of Luke is set in the context of journey. The journey serves two purposes. It is a symbol of the Christian life, and it is Jesus' movement toward his salvation destiny.

Christians are formed by the journey itself. Journey is the school where discipleship is learned. We learn what it means to live in God's reign by living in it. There are no favorites in the reign of God, nor is there a place for self-righteous smugness.

Jesus was asked who would be saved. Jews discussed this question and maintained that idolaters and brave sinners would be excluded. Jesus disapproved of the self-righteousness of some and insisted that their narrow-mindedness had no place in the reign of God.

Membership in the reign of God required repentant hearts. Period. Religious superiority, rigorous adherence to the law, and religious observance mean nothing if the person's heart is unrepentant. Sinners, tax collectors, and the unclean will enter long before the self-righteous. The implications for today's world are staggering. It demands that we ask ourselves: who are the gentiles, sinners, and the unclean in today's world? Would we welcome them as Jesus welcomed them?

Tension was mounting in the Jesus story. Many were against him. Today's Gospel seems to imply that even those who had eaten with Jesus and offered him hospitality were among the unsaved. The point is clear. Simply knowing Jesus was not enough. Would-be disciples were invited into deep personal relationship. Jesus' message is becoming more urgent, "Repent while you still have the chance." It was a time for decisive action.

Invitation to Group Sharing

1. When approaching reception of the Eucharist, am I reminded that my heart is to be open to all people?

2. Is there anyone in my life who is currently unwelcome? What will be my Christian response?

3. God invites us into deep personal relationship. In what ways have I responded (or not) to that relationship?

4. Who are the unclean, the sinners, tax collectors, and gentiles of today's world? What do I have in common with them? Who in those categories would I find difficult to welcome? What would have to change for me to welcome them? Who might find difficulty being welcomed in my or our parish? What might I, or our group, do to welcome them?

Invitation to Act

Determine a specific action (individual or group) that flows from your sharing. This should be your primary consideration. When choosing an individual action, determine what you will do and share it with the group. When choosing a group action, determine who will take responsibility for different aspects of the action. The following are secondary suggestions:

1. Determine if anyone would feel unwelcome in your parish community and make a concerted effort this week to welcome and offer hospitality to one person.

2. Pray for a change of heart when it comes to your rejection of anyone in God's family, especially in your immediate family.

3. Commit to one action this week that would counter your inhospitality of heart.

4. Pray for repentant hearts and together reach out this week to someone society has rejected.

Invitation to Closing Prayer

Give thanks to God (aloud or silently) for insights gained, for desires awakened, for directions clarified, for the gift of one another's openness and sensitivity. Conclude with the following:

God of mercy, Father of all,
you welcome the downtrodden
and are a voice for the voiceless.

You feed those who are poor
and offer forgiveness to sinners.

And above all, you sent us your Son
for the salvation of the world.

Reveal to us our unrepentant, stony hearts
and replace them
with hearts full of love and compassion.

Place your Spirit within us,
so that we might walk in your footsteps
and speak your Word to a waiting world.

Enfold us in your protective arms
and help us grow in the intimacy
you long to share with us.

We ask this through Christ our Lord. Amen.

Twenty-Second Sunday in Ordinary Time

All Are Equally Welcome

Invitation to Pray

Pause for a few moments of silence and enter more deeply into the presence of God.

Song

We Come to Your Feast
or
Song of the Body of Christ

Proclaim the Gospel

Luke 14:1, 7-14
Conduct of Invited Guests

Take a few minutes to savor a word, a phrase, a question, or a feeling that rises up in you. Reflect on this quietly or share it aloud.

The other Scripture readings of the day are

Sirach 3:17-18, 20, 28-29,
Psalm 68:4-7, 10-11,
and Hebrews 12:18-19, 22-24a.

Invitation to Reflect on the Gospel

Jesus watched the ostentatious behavior of some Pharisees at a Sabbath meal. In response, he posed a hypothetical wedding feast to challenge them. The scene opens with one guest who proceeded to a high place of honor at the wedding table, knowing that he risked being bumped to a lower place should a dignitary of higher status come to take his place. Next on the scene is another guest who proceeded to the lowest place. In the prevailing culture those who assumed lower places had nowhere to go but up. They knew that probably they would be invited to a higher place.

We are alerted to a special intimacy between the host and the guest when he called him "friend." The humble guest shared a special relationship with the host. The one who rushed to a place of honor was shamed, and the one who assumed a place of humility was honored.

Jesus then addressed his Pharisee dinner host. This is the same Pharisee who had earlier tried to trap him; Jesus was being watched and baited. Jesus challenged his host to reach out to those who are poor and outcast, those who had no chance of repaying the kindness. Believers are to respond to those who are poor because it is God's will. There would be no showy earthly rewards. Jesus chastised these Pharisees and insisted that they stop trying to earn the respect of other human beings. They should seek God's reward and God's respect.

God entered into a covenant relationship with the human race at the creation of the world. God promised to take care of us and, in return, we would take care of the weaker members of society. Jesus was reminding the Pharisees of the responsibility they had forgotten. God wills that we care for those who cannot care for themselves and those who have no means of repayment.

Jesus used a parable so his message would have wider appeal. All who listen to this parable are to put themselves in the place of the Pharisees. And if the sandal fits, they are to wear it.

The bottom line is simple. God plays no favorites. All are welcome equally. Disciples are to go out and welcome all of God's rejected children. Those who assume the lowest place at table assume the posture of Christ. The implications for disciples are clear. Can we do less?

Invitation to Group Sharing

1. Who would our society find offensive to invite to the wedding feast?

2. What kind of folks would I feel most uncomfortable inviting to the wedding feast?

3. To whom do I relate more: the guest who hurried to the place of honor, or the one who assumed the lowest place? Have I ever known anyone who is an example of either postures?

4. What can I do to reach out to the "outcasts" in my own life and in society?

Invitation to Act

Determine a specific action (individual or group) that flows from your sharing. This should be your primary consideration. When choosing an individual action, determine what you will do and share it with the group. When choosing a group action, determine who will take responsibility for different aspects of the action. The following are secondary suggestions:

1. Make a call to someone neglected and at the fringe of your life.

2. Volunteer at a homeless shelter and spend time talking to one of the people our society has rejected.

3. Make a commitment to become more aware of the marginalized and fringe members of your community. Make a conscious effort to include them in parish activities.

4. Consider being advocates for those who are homeless, or afflicted with AIDS, or others rejected by society. You might inquire with your state Catholic Conference about pending legislation that impacts powerless members of society. Inquire about becoming effective advocates.

Invitation to Closing Prayer

Give thanks to God (aloud or silently) for insights gained, for desires awakened, for directions clarified, for the gift of one another's openness and sensitivity. Conclude with the following:

Lord God,
you have created us in your image.

And through the incarnation of your Son
you have gifted them with your divinity.

You have made human beings the stewards of creation
and have gifted us with a dignity only you can give.

You have set a banquet table for all your children
and you will go to the ends of the earth
to seek out the lost,
and give them a place of honor at your divine table.

Instill in your disciples your very own passion
for the rejected of our world.

Send them out to gather the lost
and invite them to your heavenly feast.

And let this be accomplished
through the power of your Holy Spirit.

We ask this through your Son Jesus Christ,
our Lord and Savior. Amen.

Twenty-Third Sunday in Ordinary Time

Radical Discipleship

Invitation to Pray

Pause for a few moments of silence and enter more deeply into the presence of God.

Song

You Are Mine

Proclaim the Gospel

Luke 14:25-33
Sayings on Discipleship

Take a few minutes to savor a word, a phrase, a question, or a feeling that rises up in you. Reflect on this quietly or share it aloud.

The other Scripture readings of the day are

Wisdom 9:13-18b,
Psalm 90:3-6, 12-17,
and Philemon 9-10, 12-17.

Invitation to Reflect on the Gospel

Today's Gospel serves as just one more wake-up call in a series of such calls we have heard these past weeks. Jesus insists that the command to follow in his steps and to carry one's cross is a lifetime endeavor and requires diligence. The phrase "hating" one's father and mother seems harsh to us, yet the original Greek in Luke's Gospel uses that exact wording. Matthew's Gospel softened it considerably by rewording it: "Whoever loves father or mother more than me ..." (Matthew 10:37). Luke prefers to stay with the more severe version. He does not want his point to be missed. Disciples must avoid over-attachment to possessions and relationships. Nothing is to get in the way of one's relationship with God or with the mission of Christ. Absolutely nothing, absolutely no one.

Christians were experiencing serious persecution. Their Christian affiliation was beginning to cause trouble even on the home front. Jesus is exhorting his disciples to stand firm in the face of persecution, to accept the cross even when it reaches into the home environment.

In the ancient world, loyalty to the family was paramount. People seldom left the family system. Families were extremely controlling and dictated behavior. It would be difficult to resist the pressures of family dominance. Radical discipleship insists that followers of Christ let go of the security of their family ties. Jesus was well-aware of that dynamic, but insisted that such control constituted excessive attachment. Disciples cannot afford over-attachment to anything. Their lives must now be directed toward their new family—the family of God. Christianity is costly; it may even cost a people their primary relationships. No one ever suggested that carrying the cross would be easy. It requires tough choices. But the rewards are eternal.

Invitation to Group Sharing

1. How do I find a balance between the need for strong family ties and support, and the need for me to be able to stand on Christian convictions? Give examples.

2. In what ways can we strengthen the Catholic fiber of our families?

3. Is there an area of my life that Jesus is speaking to when he insists that disciples must avoid excessive attachments to relationships?

4. In what concrete way does this Gospel invite me to carry the cross?

5. What might we do to direct our lives, in a more focused way, to the family of God?

Invitation to Act

Determine a specific action (individual or group) that flows from your sharing. This should be your primary consideration. When choosing an individual action, determine what you will do and share it with the group. When choosing a group action, determine who will take responsibility for different aspects of the action. The following are secondary suggestions:

1. Take serious prayer time this week to examine specifically all your relationships. Is God really the center of your life, your relationships? Make a list of ways God is at the center of your life, and the areas where possessions and relationships take center stage.

2. Take time to assess your group and its primary focus. Is God still the center of your gathering? Does your group spend enough time in prayer?

3. One way we can place God first is to reach out to another person or persons in need. Find someone this week who needs your attention and spend some time with him or her. Perhaps you might go to a nursing home and visit someone who has no family or visitors.

Invitation to Closing Prayer

Give thanks to God (aloud or silently) for insights gained, for desires awakened, for directions clarified, for the gift of one another's openness and sensitivity. Conclude with the following:

God of the living,
all the earth bows down before you.

All creation groans in praise of you.

You alone are the Lord of lords.

You alone are the God of all creation.

You invite all human beings
into deep and personal relationship.

You insist that we shall have no other gods before you.

Help us as we seek to place you first in our lives.

Send your Spirit to strengthen us
as we strive to embrace the cross,
and fill us with the wisdom we need
to resist the attachments of this world.

Alone we can do nothing,
with you all things are possible.

This we pray through the power of Jesus' name. Amen.

TWENTY-FOURTH SUNDAY IN ORDINARY TIME

Forgive and Welcome

Invitation to Pray

Pause for a few moments of silence and enter more deeply into the presence of God.

Song

Amazing Grace

Proclaim the Gospel

Luke 15:1-10
The Lost Sheep, the Lost Coin

Take a few minutes to savor a word, a phrase, a question, or a feeling that rises up in you. Reflect on this quietly or share it aloud.

The other Scripture readings of the day are

Exodus 32:7-11, 13-14,
Psalm 51:3-4, 12-13, 17, 19,
and 1 Timothy 1:12-17.

Invitation to Reflect on the Gospel

The first line of the Gospel alerts us to an important way we are to listen to the parables. Jesus is addressing these self-righteous Pharisees who were angry he was eating with sinners. The parables challenge the religious leaders who were obviously not behaving the way Jesus believed true shepherds of the people should behave. These Pharisees were furious that Jesus was offering forgiveness and welcoming sinners into his community without demanding that they make restitution, sacrifice, and commitment to the law. "Who does Jesus think he is anyway? What makes him think he knows who God welcomes and does not welcome?" The Pharisees must have found Jesus' examples absurd. Who, in their right mind, would turn the house upside down to look for one coin, or go after one sheep and leave the others (especially when they believed the sheep was not worth saving in the first place)?

Very often the parable of the lost coin has been translated as a parable about the contrast between the rich shepherd and the poor woman. Biblical research has suggested another reality. The woman was not poor; by first century standards, she was well-off. She may have lost one drachma, a day's wage, but she had ten others—an unheard-of luxury. The two stories illustrate through a male and a female character the way God acts.

"How dare Jesus suggest that we Pharisees are like the notoriously ill-reputed shepherds and a woman—what an insult!" Yet, is that not just like God—to come as a lowly one who offers life itself? The parable invites the Pharisees and listeners of all ages to expand their image of God, and to enter more fully into God's extraordinary generosity. God moves heaven and earth to welcome sinners. The parable invites all men and women to act like God—to go to any lengths in welcoming and loving all people.

Invitation to Group Sharing

1. What does today's Gospel have to teach me about "seeking out the lost"? Focus on those close to you, family and friends, and think through how you might reach them. Give special attention to those who are

in a time of need or hurting, and how the sharing of your faith experience might move them. How can I share the good news with them?

2. Name experiences in which you behaved like some of the Pharisees (self-righteous smugness) and when you behaved like the woman and the shepherd (unconditional love and compassion). What did I learn from the experience? In what way does this Gospel invite me to concretely respond?

3. What does the Gospel mean for today's Church? How does this Gospel speak to religious leaders—clergy, religious, and laity?

Invitation to Act

Determine a specific action (individual or group) that flows from your sharing. This should be your primary consideration. When choosing an individual action, determine what you will do and share it with the group. When choosing a group action, determine who will take responsibility for different aspects of the action. The following are secondary suggestions:

1. Determine a particular person in need with whom you will share your faith story.

2. Spend some time each day reading the Scriptures looking for examples of how God reaches out to those who are lost. Each day write down an example from your life of how God has reached out to you when you were lost, or felt abandoned and rejected.

3. Perhaps your group might consider choosing a few neighborhoods and go door-to-door to welcome folks to come to your parish.

Invitation to Closing Prayer

Give thanks to God (aloud or silently) for insights gained, for desires awakened, for directions clarified, for the gift of one another's openness and sensitivity. Conclude with the following:

God of the lost,
through the Incarnation of your Son,
you free human beings from the ravages of sin,
and you pour out your abundant mercy
on the lost and the broken.

Sinners find refuge in the shadow of your wings.

And you provide your people
with an abundant harvest.

Send workers into the world
to seek out the lost
and offer life to sinners.

Direct our efforts and purify our hearts,
as we go out seeking the lost sheep of this world.

May your Spirit empower us
to become more effective ambassadors
of your compassion.

We ask this in the name of Jesus the Lord. Amen.

TWENTY-FIFTH SUNDAY IN ORDINARY TIME

Resourceful Stewarding

Invitation to Pray

Pause for a few moments of silence and enter more deeply into the presence of God.

Song

Lord, You Have Come
or
Only This I Want

Proclaim the Gospel

Luke 16:1-13
Parable of the Dishonest Steward

Take a few minutes to savor a word, a phrase, a question, or a feeling that rises up in you. Reflect on this quietly or share it aloud.

The other Scripture readings of the day are

Amos 8:4-7,
Psalm 113:1-2, 4-8,
and 1 Timothy 2:1-8.

Invitation to Reflect on the Gospel

Parables startled their listeners, captured their attention and invited conversion. Today's parable is one of the most difficult parables to understand. The listeners of this parable would have been startled by the fact that the unjust steward was not immediately jailed after he was fired. Life was, nevertheless, over for him. No one would ever hire him again.

The scene opens with the manager committing some dishonest deed and the master finding out. The manager's silence reveals his guilt. He is in trouble and he knows it; he cannot dig ditches and he will not beg. How will he support himself?

He devises a plan and decides to count on the master's generosity he had experienced earlier. In the name of the master, the manager reduces some of the renter's debt. The master would be greatly honored and praised for his generosity. He would be the talk of the village, and there would be great rejoicing. The manager was confident that the master would not put a damper on the community's joy by publicly exposing the situation. The manager's future employment possibilities would thus remain intact. He cleverly preserved his future by counting on the master's mercy.

It appears as if the manager's solution was dishonest and cut into the master's profits. That is not the case, however. The amount he deducted from the rents constituted the amount he would have added to the principle for his own commission. Jesus was exhorting his disciples to rely on God's mercy and power to save, but also to be as clever and as diligent as the steward in securing their future in the reign of God. This is a "how much more" parable. If the manager provided for his future by his clever manipulation of wealth, "how much more" will disciples do the same by using wealth to build the reign of God.

Another theme in today's Gospel suggests that anyone who is a lackadaisical steward of this world's resources can hardly be entrusted with the truths of the kingdom. Reliance on God was evidenced by the way believers were good stewards [or not] of the resources entrusted to them and how they cared for those who are poor. Disciples are to be clever stewards of all that has been entrusted to them.

Invitation to Group Sharing

1. What do I need to learn from today's Gospel? Have I ever had an experience in which honest resourcefulness helped me sort through a difficult situation? Where was the hand of God in that situation?

2. How does this Gospel invite me to use the material resources at my disposal? How do I feel about Jesus' insistence that good stewardship has as much to do with resources as it does with the Christian truth? Explain and give an example.

3. What are the implications of the challenge for me to be generous with my financial resources? How will I respond?

Invitation to Act

Determine a specific action (individual or group) that flows from your sharing. This should be your primary consideration. When choosing an individual action, determine what you will do and share it with the group. When choosing a group action, determine who will take responsibility for different aspects of the action. The following are secondary suggestions:

1. Spend some time this week reflecting on the ways in which you are a good steward of your time, talent, and treasure. Commit to work on one area that needs strengthening.

2. Determine a worthy cause to which you will extend great generosity.

3. We know that God is a God of all, especially those who are powerless. Yet, in today's Gospel, the steward seems to help himself. He was only able to help himself because of his experience of God's incredible mercy. Each night this week, look over the story of your life and reflect upon one experience in which you were able to use your own giftedness, fed by your experience of God's providence, to help you through a difficult situation in your life. Keep a journal and share the good news with a friend during the week.

4. Lobby your legislators on a key issue they are considering.

Invitation to Closing Prayer

Give thanks to God (aloud or silently) for insights gained, for desires awakened, for directions clarified, for the gift of one another's openness and sensitivity. Conclude with the following:

Compassionate and merciful God,
you adorn the earth with lush treasures
and clothe it in royal attire.

You provide human beings with every good gift
and you feed us with spiritual food.

Your compassion is endless;
your mercy flows freely like a river.

Gift us, your faithful servants,
with your wisdom and creativity,
so we may be good stewards
of the wealth you have entrusted to our care.

Strengthen us as we go forth
to share your truth with the rest of the world.

Grant this through your Son, our Lord Jesus Christ,
who lives and reigns with you and the Holy Spirit,
one God, forever and ever. Amen.

TWENTY-SIXTH SUNDAY IN ORDINARY TIME

The Poor at Our Doorstep

Invitation to Pray

Pause for a few moments of silence and enter more deeply into the presence of God.

Song
That There May Be Bread

Proclaim the Gospel

Luke 16:19-31
Parable of the Rich Man and Lazarus

Take a few minutes to savor a word, a phrase, a question, or a feeling that rises up in you. Reflect on this quietly or share it aloud.

The other Scripture readings of the day are

Amos 6:1a, 4-7,
Psalm 146:7-10,
and 1 Timothy 6:11-16.

Invitation to Reflect on the Gospel

Every one of us is the rich person in today's Gospel. There is always someone poorer than we at our doorstep. Some years ago at an international conference in the capital of a developing country, a visitor was struck by the poverty he met in that city. Orphaned street children surrounded the conference building, and poor people sat begging in the streets. He joined an exposure excursion to a slum area, and he was simply overwhelmed by the poverty.

When the conference was over after about a week or so, he was heard to say that he was very glad to go home because he would not be able to stand this confrontation with poverty all the time.

He went and escaped, in a way. Yet, he did not escape at all. He only enlarged the distance between his front door at home and those poor people. He behaved like a child, closing his eyes to a danger it fears, reasoning: "If I don't see it, it does not exist."

All of us are rich in comparison to those who are poorer than we are. That is why all of us have to listen carefully to this Gospel story. What are we being called to do?

The story tells us riches, as such, neither help in one's salvation nor in one's relations with God. It does not advise us to turn over our riches or become poor in the process.

The Gospel teaches something else. When the rich man in hell asks Abraham to send Lazarus to his five (rich) brothers, Abraham answers that they should listen to Moses and the prophets. They should listen to those who urged all of us to organize—in the name of God—a world in which everyone would feel at home, and nobody would lie at the door of someone else. We are called to invite one another into our homes and into our hearts, so that we look at each poor person as "one of us" and not "one of them." Ultimately, we are compelled to witness the suffering with others intimately.

Invitation to Group Sharing

1. Upon reflection, do I detect any insensitivity or degree of coolness in my attitude toward those who are poor?

2. Who are the poor people nearest to my front door, my office, my church, my school?

3. In what way could we transform our charitable outreach to others so that they are not only helped from moment to moment, but their situation will be changed for the future?

Invitation to Act

Determine a specific action (individual or group) that flows from your sharing. This should be your primary consideration. When choosing an individual action, determine what you will do and share it with the group. When choosing a group action, determine who will take responsibility for different aspects of the action. The following are secondary suggestions:

1. Decide on a specific action that could help change the condition of those who are poor in your area. Befriend a person who is poor in this action. Ask him or her what needs changing and how can you do it together.

2. Use your political influence, as a voter, to help those who are poor. Write letters to newspapers and attend community meetings.

3. Give the clothing and household goods you do not use or need to the St. Vincent de Paul Society or a similar organization. Keep the anonymous recipients in your prayers. Reflect on how you can do this every month, week, etc.

4. Search the newspaper for the face of a real person who is poor. Pray for him or her daily; keep his or

her story close to you, reminding you of God's
radical call to servanthood.

Invitation to Closing Prayer

*Give thanks to God (aloud or silently) for insights
gained, for desires awakened, for directions clarified,
for the gift of one another's openness and sensitivity.
Conclude with the following, praying it together at least
twice:*

Lead us, Lord God,
on this day that we are invited
to be aware of the misery of others,
to live our common humanity
respecting others,
offering them what they need,
and willing to review our own priorities.

We make our prayer through Christ our Lord. Amen.

TWENTY-SEVENTH SUNDAY IN ORDINARY TIME

Like a Seed

Invitation to Pray

Pause for a few moments of silence and enter more deeply into the presence of God.

Song
> We Thank You, Father

Proclaim the Gospel
> *Luke 17:5-10*
> Signs of Faith

Take a few minutes to savor a word, a phrase, a question, or a feeling that rises up in you. Reflect on this quietly or share it aloud.

The other Scripture readings of the day are

> *Habakkuk 1:2-3; 2:2-4,*
> *Psalm 95:1-2, 6-9,*
> *and 2 Timothy 1:6-8, 13-14.*

Invitation to Reflect on the Gospel

The disciples came to Jesus and they said, "Increase our faith" (v. 5) and we will work wonders, implying that at that moment their faith was so small that they could not do a thing.

They were like a farmer who says, "I don't have enough seed to sow all my land; I'll wait until I have some more and then I'll start." But he never got any more seed, and he passed away while waiting.

Jesus, in a way, does not listen to their request. He neither promises nor gives them any more faith. He tells them, "Start with the little you have and you will accomplish all you want."

He exposed in them, as he unmasks in us, one of the ways we use to escape our responsibilities. We cannot pray because we do not have sufficient faith; we cannot be charitable because we are weak Christians; we cannot organize ourselves in view of justice because we do not have sufficient data, and so on.

Jesus objects, "Don't speak like that, work with what you have. Even if your faith would be small like a mustard seed, you can work wonders."

Dorothy Day, whose beatification process was introduced by Cardinal O'Connor of New York some time ago, started all kinds of activities during her life: a newspaper, *The Catholic Worker*; homes for street people; feeding programs for those who were hungry; and even communal farms.

Many came to visit her. Sometimes she would overhear those visitors saying of her, "She is a saint!" She then would turn to them and respond, "You only say that I am a saint to convince yourself that you are different from me, that you would not be able to do the things I do. I am not different from you. You could do what I do."

You do not need any more faith than you have. Just use the faith you have!

Invitation to Group Sharing

1. What are some challenges in life I currently face that call me to greater faith?

2. What are some reasons I use to excuse myself from doing good work, telling myself that I do not have sufficient faith in God to do it?

3. In what ways do I consider people around me, who engage in all kinds of good works, as different from myself?

4. What people do I know who worked "miracles" because of their faith in the power of Jesus? What enabled them to do this? What will I, or we, do to work "miracles"?

Invitation to Act

Determine a specific action (individual or group) that flows from your sharing. This should be your primary consideration. When choosing an individual action, determine what you will do and share it with the group. When choosing a group action, determine who will take responsibility for different aspects of the action. The following are secondary suggestions:

1. Reconsider any task you might have put on hold because of a lack of faith and determine to take on the task.

2. Take a walk in a park or nearby forest, pick a large tree, consider how it grew from a small seed. Pray for a deeper faith. Ask yourself why Jesus used it as a symbol for your faith.

3. Encourage, over the coming week, someone who shows signs of discouragement or depression by pointing out the good he or she does. Keep in touch with the person, calling attention to his or her improvement in spirit, or if none, your own struggle with discouragement.

Invitation to Closing Prayer

Give thanks to God (aloud or silently) for insights gained, for desires awakened, for directions clarified, for the gift of one another's openness and sensitivity. Conclude with the following, to be said by each one individually in turn:

Loving God and Father,
my life and support,
let me grow in faith,
and let me realize that my faith in you
is nothing in comparison
to your faith in me.

Then pray together:

**We ask this in the name of Jesus, our Brother,
who lives with you and the Holy Spirit,
one God, forever and ever. Amen.**

TWENTY-EIGHTH SUNDAY IN ORDINARY TIME

Skin-Deep Only?

Invitation to Pray

Pause for a few moments of silence and enter more deeply into the presence of God.

Song

We Were Strangers
or
Eye Has Not Seen

Proclaim the Gospel

Luke 17:11-19
The Cleansing of Ten Lepers

Take a few minutes to savor a word, a phrase, a question, or a feeling that rises up in you. Reflect on this quietly or share it aloud.

The other Scripture readings of the day are

2 Kings 5:14-17,
Psalm 98:1-4,
and 2 Timothy 2:8-13.

Invitation to Reflect on the Gospel

There is a good reason to suggest that the Gospel story about the Samaritan who returned to Jesus after his healing, while the nine other lepers did not, is about thankfulness. Even Jesus asked, "Ten were cleansed, were they not? Where are the other nine" (v. 17)?

Of course, he knew where they were. It is not so difficult to guess. After having obtained their health certificates from the authorities in Jerusalem, they went home, and they went to their old jobs.

One had been a farmer, and he was milking his goats again. Another one was back in his shop doing the accounts. Others were seen drinking with their friends. But only one returned to give thanks.

Jesus had touched them all. He had healed their skin, the surface of their bodies, but their faith had not changed. Now and then they would tell their story, but that was about it.

Only the Samaritan, the stranger and outsider, came back. He fell at Jesus' feet. Jesus told him, "Stand up and go; your faith has saved you." (v. 19) or as we read in other translations, "Your faith has made you well."

Jesus was not speaking about the Samaritan's skin, but about him, about his heart, about his person, about his mind. Number ten came back; he did not return to his old life and his own world. He started a new one based on faith in Jesus.

He, too, touches us, otherwise we would not be here together reflecting on his words. But how deep does it go? When are we like the nine? When are we like the tenth person?

Invitation to Group Sharing

1. How do I respond when someone does not thank me for doing a good deed? Does another's lack of response discourage me?

2. When am I sincerely grateful for the way Jesus touches and heals me, or when do I take those aspects of my life more or less for granted?

3. Do I tend to pass off God's providential care in my life as "good luck"? How will I express thankfulness in a way that is a faith response?

4. In the Gospel story, Jesus meets a stranger. He treats him like he does his companions. He includes others in his approach. How can I be more inclusive and open to strangers?

Invitation to Act

Determine a specific action (individual or group) that flows from your sharing. This should be your primary consideration. When choosing an individual action, determine what you will do and share it with the group. When choosing a group action, determine who will take responsibility for different aspects of the action. The following are secondary suggestions:

1. Thank each person in the group for the way each one is a gift.

2. This week, give a tangible token of appreciation to someone you have been taking for granted for too long.

3. Spend sufficient prayer time to take stock of God's providential care in your life and express gratitude.

4. Become a person of gratitude! Make a list of people you have failed to give thanks to and write or phone one each week.

Invitation to Closing Prayer

Give thanks to God (aloud or silently) for insights gained, for desires awakened, for directions clarified, for the gift of one another's openness and sensitivity. Conclude with the following, to be said together three times:

Almighty God,
I am grateful to you for my existence.

I am sorry for the complaints
you often hear from me.

In fact, "my cup runneth over." *(see Psalm 23)*

Help me to live your gift of life
to the fullest each day of my life. Amen.

TWENTY-NINTH SUNDAY IN ORDINARY TIME

Perseverance

Invitation to Pray

Pause for a few moments of silence and enter more deeply into the presence of God.

Song

We Are Called
or
O Lord, Hear My Prayer

Proclaim the Gospel

Luke 18:1-8
Parable of the Persistent Widow

Take a few minutes to savor a word, a phrase, a question, or a feeling that rises up in you. Reflect on this quietly or share it aloud.

The other Scripture readings of the day are

Exodus 17:8-13,
Psalm 121:1-8,
and 2 Timothy 3:14—4:2.

Invitation to Reflect on the Gospel

Luke tells us why Jesus told the story about the persistent widow. It is to illustrate our need to pray always and not to lose heart. That widow definitely did not lose heart when she went again and again to the judge in search of justice.

The judge in the story of Jesus was so powerful, so rich, and so well protected, that he did not fear any human being. He had sufficient money and sufficient information to silence anybody. He was, so said Jesus, not even afraid of God. It is suggested that he might just have been waiting for a bribe.

When that widow came asking him again and again to do justice to her, he gave up. He said: "While it is true that I neither fear God nor respect any human being, because this widow keeps bothering me I shall deliver a just decision for her lest she finally come and strike me" (v. 4). In fact the Greek text uses a verb that indicates that he was afraid that the widow might give him a black eye or knock him out.

Jesus tells us to persevere in prayer. Let us be persistent in prayer for a troubled son or daughter; for the grace to sustain the caring of a sick child or an aging parent; for family peace and harmony; for an end of violence in our world, that justice might be done here on earth. We not only need to pray, we also have to live in a way consistent with our prayers.

Invitation to Group Sharing

1. What worthy needs can I be praying for more persistently and faithfully?

2. Why do I, at times, procrastinate in helping others?

3. How are we willing, as a group, to use the influence we have in our parish or broader community, especially when others appeal to us to help them in their predicaments.

4. What caring action will I, or we, undertake that calls for fortitude and perseverance?

Invitation to Act

Determine a specific action (individual or group) that flows from your sharing. This should be your primary consideration. When choosing an individual action, determine what you will do and share it with the group. When choosing a group action, determine who will take responsibility for different aspects of the action. The following are secondary suggestions:

1. Determine a specific need for which you will pray with persistence.

2. Let us take care that well-specified prayers for justice and peace are offered at the Prayers of the Faithful during the eucharistic celebrations.

3. Today's widows, widowers, and orphans are often considered the "outsiders" in our society and even in parish contexts. Some of them, who cannot leave their homes anymore, or do not dare to do so, are sometimes called "shut-ins." Let us try to identify them in our parish community and determine a specific way to reach out with a helping hand.

Invitation to Closing Prayer

Give thanks to God (aloud or silently) for insights gained, for desires awakened, for directions clarified, for the gift of one another's openness and sensitivity. Conclude with the following:

Almighty God,
we remember before you
all those among us who are treated unjustly,
especially ...
(Pause and name those you would like to remember.)

Bless and guide us,
that your love may be shown
in our concern for them.

In the name of Jesus we pray! Amen.

THIRTIETH SUNDAY IN ORDINARY TIME

Self-Righteousness

Invitation to Pray

Pause for a few moments of silence and enter more deeply into the presence of God.

Song

Here I am, Lord
or
Gather Us In

Proclaim the Gospel

Luke 18:9-14
Parable of the Pharisee and the Tax Collector

Take a few minutes to savor a word, a phrase, a question, or a feeling that rises up in you. Reflect on this quietly or share it aloud.

The other Scripture readings of the day are

Sirach 35:12-14, 16-18,
Psalm 34:2-3, 17-19, 23,
and 2 Timothy 4:6-8, 16-18.

Invitation to Reflect on the Gospel

Everybody knows today's Gospel. It is a simple story. Two people went to the temple. One was a Pharisee, the other a tax collector. The Pharisee was self-righteous and looked down upon others with contempt. We do not have to retell the story. We just heard it.

We usually decide that the Pharisee was a hypocrite. But Jesus did not say that. The Pharisee went wrong in something else. He gloried in himself. He told himself why God should respect and love him. He, not God, was the center of his prayer. He prayed, "O God, I thank you that I..." (v. 11). He said to himself, "O God, look at all I do for you. I am no sinner. I fast. I pay temple tax," implying, "O God look at me, a wonderful performer. You should respect me, you should love me!"

It is here that he was mistaken. Love and respect are things that are neither bought nor sold. The Pharisee turned the world upside down. He mistook the path of God's love. It is God's love from which all arises. God's love started the Pharisee's life, as it did ours. God's love is our source, our beginning. We should be pious, devout, and righteous like the Pharisee; we do this not to ask God to love us, but because God already loves us.

The tax collector already understood this. He left the initiative to God. He said, "God, let it come from you! Have mercy on me! Let it start from you!" He went home, as Jesus told us, justified, unlike the Pharisee. The tax collector understood the nature of God's love. How do I understand God's love? Am I like the Pharisee or the tax collector in my heart today?

Invitation to Group Sharing

1. Have I ever thought I needed to earn God's love? If so, who or what helped me to know I am unconditionally loved by God just as I am?

2. When an accident, a sickness, a failure, a loss of a job, etc., strikes me, do I see this as an injustice from God? Share your experience.

3. In our conversations how do we refer to those who do not belong to our group or even to our religion? How would we be able to overcome any exclusive attitude?

Invitation to Act

Determine a specific action (individual or group) that flows from your sharing. This should be your primary consideration. When choosing an individual action, determine what you will do and share it with the group. When choosing a group action, determine who will take responsibility for different aspects of the action. The following are secondary suggestions:

1. Enter a church or chapel this week, staying in the back and praying for some time as the tax collector did in Jesus' parable.

2. Spend some time in humble conversation with someone you may have offended through your superior attitude.

3. Take a piece of paper, draw a line in the middle of it from top to bottom, and write on the left side your good qualities, and the other side your bad ones. Acknowledge, accept, and embrace yourself in gratitude.

Invitation to Closing Prayer

Give thanks to God (aloud or silently) for insights gained, for desires awakened, for directions clarified, for the gift of one another's openness and sensitivity. Pray the following, singing it together "recto tono," that is, on one note:

Dear Jesus,
you are like a mirror
in which we can see ourselves

with our limits and our possibilities.

Teach us to see ourselves
as loved by you completely
just as we are. Amen.

THIRTY-FIRST SUNDAY IN ORDINARY TIME

Zacchaeus

Invitation to Pray

Pause for a few moments of silence and enter more deeply into the presence of God.

Song

Only This I Want

Proclaim the Gospel

Luke 19:1-10
Zacchaeus the Tax Collector

Take a few minutes to savor a word, a phrase, a question, or a feeling that rises up in you. Reflect on this quietly or share it aloud.

The other Scripture readings of the day are

Wisdom 11:22–12:2,
Psalm 145:1–2, 8-11, 13, 14,
and 2 Thessalonians 1:11–2:2.

Invitation to Reflect on the Gospel

Zacchaeus was hated in Jericho. He was a collaborator of the Roman Occupational Forces. He was their tax collector. No wonder that he could not get through the crowd. He wanted to see Jesus, so he climbed a sycamore tree.

Zacchaeus was a sinner. He knew that. Maybe he knew it too well, and so did the crowd that got upset when Jesus decided to be his guest. To consider that he was no good at all was impossible for Jesus, who knew that his Father had created Zacchaeus. There was goodness in Zacchaeus that nobody would be able to take away. There was goodness in Zacchaeus that was placed there by God.

It is this goodness that never will be undone. It is this goodness Jesus came to reveal in Zacchaeus and in us. We should never forget this goodness that will last as long as human life lasts. Thomas Merton called it the *point vierge*, the "virginal point" in us. The virginal point is a presence that no one can destroy. You can disconnect yourself from any contact, but God remains present. God is there, always and everywhere.

It is this positive good Jesus called forth in Zacchaeus. It is this positive good in and around us we should call forth in others.

If we only stress the negative, the goodness might get lost, but not in the sense that it will be no longer there. When we stray from our goodness, we are like a lost key, a lost driver's license, lost money; they are all still somewhere, we only forgot where we placed them.

Jesus came to find this goodness, and once found in Zacchaeus, it blossomed immediately. While they were sitting at table, Jesus may have taken a piece of roasted lamb, but then hesitated. Was he not eating from the table of the poor? Was he not dealing in stolen goods? Zacchaeus may have seen his hesitation and he said, "I will repay all the injustices I have done; you can eat in peace." That is what Jesus did—he who had come to find what was lost.

Invitation to Group Sharing

1. What nurtures goodness in people?

2. When or what helps goodness blossom in me?

3. How do I relate to those I consider to be sinners? How can I call forth their goodness?

4. In order to be whole and healthy beings, we need to know ourselves. In what ways do I shy away from criticism because I am afraid to know? What will I bring to prayer this week?

Invitation to Act

Determine a specific action (individual or group) that flows from your sharing. This should be your primary consideration. When choosing an individual action, determine what you will do and share it with the group. When choosing a group action, determine who will take responsibility for different aspects of the action. The following are secondary suggestions:

1. Spend some time in prayer this week, allowing God to touch your core. Plan to receive the sacrament of reconciliation.

2. Share with one or two others how you see their core of goodness expressed. Do this first in prayer followed with a telephone call, visit, letter, e-mail, etc.

3. There is an annual national collection for the Catholic Campaign for Human Development. Take care that it receives the attention it deserves.

4. Consider the possibility of adopting as a community, or as an individual, a poor immigrant family, or someone else in need.

Invitation to Closing Prayer

Give thanks to God (aloud or silently) for insights gained, for desires awakened, for directions clarified, for the gift of one another's openness and sensitivity. Let one person say aloud the following, and let the others respond with "Amen" after each line:

Lord Jesus, you called Zacchaeus by his name,   **Amen.**

and you helped him to grow.   **Amen.**

Enter our lives in that way today,   **Amen.**

calling us by our names,   **Amen.**

so that we may grow   **Amen.**

and be the persons you call us to be.   **Amen.**

THIRTY-SECOND SUNDAY IN ORDINARY TIME

The Living Dead

Invitation to Pray

Pause for a few moments of silence and enter more deeply into the presence of God.

Song
We Shall Rise Again

Proclaim the Gospel

Luke 20:27-38
The Question about Resurrection

Take a few minutes to savor a word, a phrase, a question, or a feeling that rises up in you. Reflect on this quietly or share it aloud.

The other Scripture readings of the day are

2 Maccabees 7:1-2, 9-14,
Psalm 17:1, 5-6, 8, 15,
and 2 Thessalonians 2:16—3:5.

Invitation to Reflect on the Gospel

They came to ask Jesus about life after death. The ones who came to ask him did not believe in it. In fact, they came to ridicule the idea, trying to make a laughingstock of Jesus.

Jesus did believe in it. Had not the prophet Isaiah said, in the name of God,

"Can a mother forget her infant,
be without tenderness for the child of her womb?

Even should she forget,
 I will never forget you" (Isaiah 49:15).

Had not Isaiah written, in the name of the almighty God,

"See, upon the palms of my hands I have
 written your name" (Isaiah 49:16).

Jesus referred in his answer to the nature of love. He reminded them of four people they knew: Abraham, Isaac, Jacob, and Moses. He queried them, "Do you really think that God allowed those four to disappear into clouds of nothingness, into the dark of oblivion? Do you really think that God, who loved them so much, who influenced their existence so much, would have forgotten those great men even you remember? Do you really think that God is a God of dead people only? That they were like some green wood that dried up to be thrown away in a fire to turn into dust and ashes? Do you really think that God will disavow, overlook, or forget them?"

Would that not be absurd? Would that not be unbelievable? Can we think of ourselves as going to be overlooked in the end, after all our struggles, our frustrations, our moments of happiness, our moments of greatness? You must be kidding!

Mentioning the names of Abraham, Isaac, Jacob, and Moses, Jesus notes something else. He promises that those who are judged worthy will have eternal life! The life that awaits us hereafter has to do with the life here on earth. It is its consequence. We should be here on earth living worthy lives in the line of Abraham and Sarah, Isaac and Rebecca, Jacob and Rachel, Moses and of our Lord Jesus Christ, and we will live forever and ever. Amen.

Invitation to Group Sharing

1. Share the hopefulness that the thought of life everlasting gives you.

2. How do I think others will remember me after my death?

3. How would I complete the following line of poetry: "If I should die, think only this of me ... " (Rupert Brooke, "The Soldier")?

4. Comment on what movie star, Steve McQueen (1930-1980), famous for his role in the war film, *The Great Escape*, said the last year of life: "I expect to win my battle against cancer, but no matter how it goes, I am at peace with God—and so I can't lose."

Invitation to Act

Determine a specific action (individual or group) that flows from your sharing. This should be your primary consideration. When choosing an individual action, determine what you will do and share it with the group. When choosing a group action, determine who will take responsibility for different aspects of the action. The following are secondary suggestions:

1. Take your children or grandchildren to visit the grave of one of your deceased family members. Share with the children what you know about this person from your family. In family prayer, call upon the intercession of the deceased person.

2. Organize a Mass of Resurrection for all those who died in your parish since All Souls Day last November, and invite their family members to attend.

3. Have a look at your last will and testament (if you have none as yet, prepare one) and see whether your interest in the reign of God is honored. Reflect

upon whether those who are poor and those on the margin of society are taken into account.

4. Examine through whom and what experiences Jesus has revealed himself to you in your journey. Offer a prayer of thanksgiving for these people and experiences.

Invitation to Closing Prayer

Give thanks to God (aloud or silently) for insights gained, for desires awakened, for directions clarified, for the gift of one another's openness and sensitivity. Say the following together, filling in your name where indicated:

Loving Father,
in death, our lives are changed not ended.

Let us remember in word and deed
that you are calling us by name *(say your name)*
that our lives on earth
relate to our lives in heaven.

We make our prayer
through Christ our Lord. Amen.

THIRTY-THIRD SUNDAY IN ORDINARY TIME

Our Endurance Will Prevail

Invitation to Pray

Pause for a few moments of silence and enter more deeply into the presence of God.

Song

Do Not Fear To Hope
or
Mine Eyes Have Seen the Glory

Proclaim the Gospel

Luke 21:5-19
Destruction of the Temple

Take a few minutes to savor a word, a phrase, a question, or a feeling that rises up in you. Reflect on this quietly or share it aloud.

The other Scripture readings of the day are

Malachi 3:19-20a,
Psalm 98:5-9,
and 2 Thessalonians 3:7-12.

Invitation to Reflect on the Gospel

We are almost at the end of a liturgical year. The last days of a year always lead to evaluations, surveys and reports on activities, on successes and failures. Jesus gives us today a report on the last days. It seems that all will go wrong: revolutions, fights of nations against nations, kingdoms against kingdoms, earthquakes, plague, famine, signs from heaven, arrests, persecutions, interrogations, betrayals, and even executions. To offset all the grimness of this litany, when his disciples point to the temple with its white and gold glittering in the sun, Jesus simply says, "there will not be left a stone upon another stone…" (v. 6).

He also explains that the end has to do with his appearance, with the moment that he will say: "'I am he,' and, 'The time has come'" (v. 8). Here are quite good reasons to project that coming at the end of time. Many did this on December 31 in the year 999. The old basilica of Saint Peter in Rome was filled with people in sackcloth and ashes expecting a sudden end to the world. And we all remember how many expected the same end to the world again at the beginning of the third millennium. According to these expectations, the end is supposed to come as a one instant bang, with Jesus appearing saying: "'I am he,' and, 'The time has come'" (v. 8).

Yet, Jesus speaks about endurance and perseverance. Those words do not refer to just a moment. They refer to something that takes time, something that lasts. The end will surely come. Jesus did already say, "'I am he,' and, 'The time has come'" (v. 8). He sowed the seed, he lit the light, he put the yeast in the dough and the salt in the world. It is now the time of development, of growth, of fermentation. The end to all this will surely come notwithstanding all kinds of difficulties. It implies cooperation.

In our society, we have difficulties with a slowly oncoming end. We have to change, developing endurance and perseverance. So much still has to change. We are far from the end. But, by our perseverance and God's grace, we will secure our lives in the end.

Invitation to Group Sharing

1. In what ways can I be more patient in allowing God's grace to work in my life?

2. Jesus speaks about endurance and perseverance. What time or event of my life called for these virtues?

3. What kind of a prayer commitment could we, as a small community, make to ask the Lord's blessings upon our ministry or our community? (For example, to pray at noontime each day for other members of the community, to pray the Hail Mary or one decade of the rosary each day for our ministry.)

Invitation to Act

Determine a specific action (individual or group) that flows from your sharing. This should be your primary consideration. When choosing an individual action, determine what you will do and share it with the group. When choosing a group action, determine who will take responsibility for different aspects of the action. The following are secondary suggestions:

1. Spend some time in prayer thinking about your own death. Is there anything you would like to do before you die? Be open to whatever inspirations the Spirit gives you.

2. Join the bereavement ministry in your parish. If one does not exist, speak with others about the possibility of starting one.

3. Become part of a hospice ministry.

Invitation to Closing Prayer

Give thanks to God (aloud or silently) for insights gained, for desires awakened, for directions clarified, for the gift of one another's openness and sensitivity. As one member prays each prayer line, all respond, "Lord, have mercy":

Let us pray,
for peace in the world,
for those who are in prison for the sake of justice,
for those who suffer because of natural disasters,
for those who are sick because of pollution,
for those who are upset
because of their fear for the future,
for children who are abused in their homes
or place of work,
for those who forget us,
for those who love us
and for those who hate us. Amen.

Last Sunday
in Ordinary Time

Christ, the King

Invitation to Pray

Pause for a few moments of silence and enter more deeply into the presence of God.

Song

Bring Forth the Kingdom
or
Jesus Remember Me

Proclaim the Gospel

Luke 23:35-43
The Crucifixion

Take a few minutes to savor a word, a phrase, a question, or a feeling that rises up in you. Reflect on this quietly or share it aloud.

The other Scripture readings of the day are

2 Samuel 5:1-3,
Psalm 122:1-5,
and Colossians 1:12-20.

Invitation to Reflect on the Gospel

Today's Gospel brings us to Jesus' most painful and apparently most powerless moment in his life. He hung on the cross between two murderers. A crown of thorns lay on his head, and, to explain the reason for his execution, the soldiers put a notice above his head: "King of the Jews."

The sky was overcast. Jesus shouted for God; he asked for water. He watched as his clothing was carried away. All glory seemed lost; he hung there naked. All dreams had ended; all hope was squashed; faith in him was gone; his disciples were on the run; and Mary and some women who followed him, were kept at a distance.

The crowd around him was shouting at him: "If you are the King of the Jews, save yourself" (v. 37). One of the two murderers joined their jeers. He, too, shouted, "Are you not the Messiah? Save yourself and us" (v. 39). The second murderer shouted at the first one, "Have you no fear of God, for you are subject to the same condemnation? And indeed, we have been condemned justly, for the sentence we received corresponds to our crimes, but this man has done nothing criminal" (vv. 40-41). Then turning his head to Jesus, he said, "Jesus, remember me when you come into your kingdom" (v. 42).

Jesus turned with his very last bit of strength. He had found a companion, a new beginning, and a stepping stone into his kingdom. He says, "Amen I say to you, today you will be with me in Paradise" (v. 43). He is, he was, and he will be king. There, on the cross, all this was manifested by his acceptance of the person next to him, who believed in his kingdom and asked him to be his companion.

Imagine how our world would change if we said to Jesus, "Remember me, I want to be with you." Our hearts would change. We would discover him in each other. His reign would work over us. So be it!

It is faith like the thief's that builds the bridge between here and there, the bridge between now and then. And with that conclusion, we are ready to be on the lookout for Christ again, to start a new year with him as our King.

Invitation to Group Sharing

1. Where, when, and how do I carry Christ's cross in my life?

2. Share a time of finding strength when confronted with someone's need to be helped, or when faced with the weakness and vulnerability of someone else.

3. Share your impressions of the many feelings Mary must have experienced standing at the foot of the cross.

4. Who in our community are those who carry Jesus' cross at the moment? What can I, or we, do to help them?

Invitation to Act

Determine a specific action (individual or group) that flows from your sharing. This should be your primary consideration. When choosing an individual action, determine what you will do and share it with the group. When choosing a group action, determine who will take responsibility for different aspects of the action. The following are secondary suggestions:

1. Place a crucifix prominently in your home, if you do not have one already.

2. Wear a medal or crucifix to remind you of Jesus' suffering and your own. Call forth Jesus throughout your day to be with you, touching your medal or crucifix.

3. Reflectively pray the Sorrowful Mysteries of the rosary.

4. Pope John Paul II and the Catholic bishops in this country have expressed their opposition to the death penalty. Join them in their appeal.

5. Check whether the parish community buildings and the church are welcoming those who are disabled regarding accessibility, bathrooms, sign language, and hearing aids. If not, begin to do something about it.

Invitation to Closing Prayer

Give thanks to God (aloud or silently) for insights gained, for desires awakened, for directions clarified, for the gift of one another's openness and sensitivity. Conclude with the following:

Lord Jesus,
let your presence in my life
and the power of your Spirit
transform me and enable me
to choose living your kingdom
in my day and age,
and help me remember
that I live in that presence
and with that Spirit. Amen.

SOLEMNITIES AND FEASTS
AND THE SUNDAY CELEBRATION

There are 11 solemnities and feasts that occur on fixed days of the year and that supersede the Eucharistic liturgy of the day when they fall on a Sunday. Faith-sharing sessions for these solemnities and feasts are provided in this appendix. The Solemnity of the Ascension of the Lord, traditionally the fortieth day of Easter, replaces the Seventh Sunday of Easter each year in many dioceses. The Solemnity of the Ascension is included in the Easter Season in this book.

MARY, MOTHER OF GOD

January 1

Mary's Role as First Disciple

Invitation to Pray

Pause for a few moments of silence to enter more deeply into the presence of God.

Song

Hail Mary, Gentle Woman

Proclaim the Gospel

Luke 2:16-21
The Visit of the Shepherds

Take a few minutes to savor a word, a phrase, a question, or a feeling that rises up in you. Reflect on this quietly or share it aloud.

The other Scripture readings of the day are

Numbers 6:22-27,
Psalm 67:2-3, 5-6, 8,
and Galatians 4:4-7.

Invitation to Reflect on the Gospel

Mary gives birth in a barn or stable and the shepherds come to see her Child. They leave singing praises. Mary ponders and reflects and treasures all these things that happen to her. She is our model in so many ways. Here, Mary is the first follower of Jesus, the first disciple. And the example she sets, the model she gives through her actions, is that a follower of Jesus takes time to reflect on life's events. A true disciple believes that there is meaning and mystery in daily life. A Christian takes time to pray quietly and sit at the feet of his or her Master to be still and hear God's lessons that present themselves.

What can I learn from this? What is this teaching me? What is God's message? These are questions we can ask each day as we meditate on the happenings of our seemingly ordinary life. There is always another dimension in which we live. The spiritual is real, but hidden.

And the way to uncover it is simply to ponder, as did Mary, and ask God to help us see with eyes of faith the important meaning, message, and challenge that we might otherwise miss. This is the role of a disciple as Mary, the first disciple, shows us. We, too, must ponder, reflect, and treasure the gifts of each day that God gives us.

Invitation to Group Sharing

1. What value would I find in following Mary's example of reflection? When in my life has that proved valuable?

2. How do I take time to listen in my heart each day, as Mary does? How could I alter my schedule to make more time? Is there someone who would help me keep such a commitment? Is there a quiet place I can go?

3. Perhaps our parish has or could provide a group setting for Marian prayer and regular reflection, or help us to learn how to do this kind of reflection better. Is there a way we might bring this about?

Invitation to Act

Determine a specific action (individual or group) that flows from your sharing. This should be your primary consideration. When choosing an individual action, determine what you will do and share it with the group. When choosing a group action, determine who will take responsibility for different aspects of the action. The following are secondary suggestions:

1. Tell another person of your commitment to reflect regularly and ask him or her to pray for you each day at that time. Offer to do the same for that person.

2. Join a group that does regular reflective prayer to become more comfortable with it yourself.

3. Read a book on Christian meditation to become more skilled and confident in your commitment, for example, Thomas Keating's *Open Mind, Open Heart.*

Invitation to Closing Prayer

Give thanks to God (aloud or silently) for insights gained, for desires awakened, for directions clarified, for the gift of one another's openness and sensitivity. Conclude with the following:

Mary, you are the Mother of Jesus and our Mother,
our guide and inspiration.
Although we see your life as extraordinary,
you lived each day as an ordinary person
in your own time and place.

Help us to live our ordinary lives according to God's will.
Help us to see God's will
and the connections between the ordinary
   and extraordinary
that exist for us each day.

Give us the commitment to ponder and
  savor life as you did.
Bless us with insight to recognize
the Spirit's action in our lives
and reflect the Father's goodness to others.
We ask this in the name of Jesus, your Son. Amen.

FEAST OF THE PRESENTATION OF THE LORD

February 2

"The Favor of God was upon Him"

Invitation to Pray

Pause for a few moments of silence to enter more deeply into the presence of God.

Song

Sing of Mary, Meek and Lowly

Proclaim the Gospel

Luke 2:22-40

"And you yourself a sword will pierce"

Take a few minutes to savor a word, a phrase, a question, or a feeling that rises up in you. Reflect on this quietly or share it aloud.

The other Scripture readings of the day are

Malachi: 3:1-4
Psalm: 24:7, 8, 9, 10 (10b)
and Hebrews: 2:14-18

Invitation to Reflect on the Gospel

This feast commemorates the first appearance of the Holy Family in the Temple in Jerusalem. On the occasion St. Luke describes, Mary, although perpetually a virgin, underwent the ritual purification required of the mother of a firstborn son. In fact, for centuries, this feast was known as the Purification of the Blessed Virgin. Mary and Joseph also brought Jesus to the Temple to dedicate him to the Lord, a stipulation of the Law of Moses. Eventually, that became the focus, and the feast became known as the Presentation of the Lord.

The presentation has been called the "second epiphany." The appearance of the infant Jesus in the Temple evokes the prophecy of Malachi: "See, I am sending my messenger to prepare the way before me, and the Lord whom you seek will suddenly come to his temple" (Malachi 3:1). John the Baptist had been born only several months before, and already the Savior John was to announce appeared in God's house. Nor did the arrival of Jesus go unnoticed; it was indeed an epiphany for Anna and Simeon, who heralded the child who would redeem not only Israel, whose expectation these prayerful people embodied, but the whole world. Simeon's reference to Jesus as a "light of revelation to the Gentiles" inspired Pope Sergius I in the eighth century to add to the rituals of this feast a procession that included the blessing and distribution of candles. That practice is still observed in some places, and the feast is sometimes referred to as Candlemas.

A striking feature of Luke's account is the exuberant prayer of Simeon, "Master, you are now dismissing your servant in peace . . . for my eyes have seen your salvation." This song of gratitude has resonated through the ages, and the Church still repeats it daily at the conclusion of Night Prayer in *The Liturgy of the Hours*.

But there also was an ominous note. Simeon told Mary, "This child is destined for the falling and the rising of many in Israel, and to be a sign that will be opposed so that the inner thoughts of many will be revealed—and a sword will pierce your own soul too." There was nothing like this in the messages of the archangel who told Mary that she would bear a son conceived by the Holy Spirit nor in the angel's counsel to Joseph to proceed without fear to take Mary into his home. Mary and Joseph accepted the angel's word because they believed it to be God's will. And then, hearing from a holy man in the Temple that their son's work would inspire resistance and that Mary herself would feel the effects of the opposition to him, the couple still accepted God's will and continued with love to carry out their responsibilities as parents of this holy child.

Invitation to Group Sharing

1. What emotions do you think Mary and Joseph were feeling as they listened to Anna and Simeon speaking about Jesus?

2. Do the challenges and troubles in life sometimes seem to contradict the promises of the Gospel? In what ways?

3. What helps you to accept challenges and deal with troubles and yet remain confident in the Lord's promises?

Invitation to Act

Determine a specific action (individual or group) that flows from your sharing. This should be your primary consideration. When choosing an individual action, determine what you will do and share it with the group. When choosing a group action, determine who will take responsibility for different aspects of the action. The following are secondary suggestions:

1. Identify an individual or group of people in your community—a frail or disabled neighbor, residents of a nursing home, prisoners—for whom the difficulties of life may make the promise of salvation

seem remote or contradictory. Offer your companionship and your own faith experiences as means through which such people can regain hope.

2. If your parish does not have a babysitting service that allows young parents to attend Mass while their infants or toddlers are being well cared for nearby, research such programs in other parishes and suggest a plan to your pastor or parish council.

3. If your parish does not have a Candlemas procession on this feast, research the background and meaning of the practice and propose it to your pastor or to the parish liturgy committee. Emphasize the opportunity to present Jesus as the light to all people.

Invitation to Closing Prayer

Give thanks to God (aloud or silently) for insights gained, for desires awakened, for directions clarified, for the gift of one another's openness and sensitivity. Conclude with the following:

All: **Almighty God, you have shown the Savior to the world
in the announcements of an angel,
in the prophecies of Anna and Simeon,
in the proclamations of John the Baptism,
in the Lord's own ministry,
sacrifice, resurrection, and ascension into heaven.**

**May we to whom he has been revealed
patiently endure life's challenges,
and faithfully live according to his example
and his Gospel of love.**

**We ask this through our Lord, Jesus Christ,
who lives and reigns with you and the Holy Spirit,
one God, forever and ever. Amen**

FEAST OF THE NATIVITY OF JOHN THE BAPTIST

June 24

"The child grew and became strong in spirit"

Invitation to Pray

Pause for a few moments of silence to enter more deeply into the presence of God.

Song

On Jordan's Bank

Proclaim the Gospel

Luke 1:57-66,80

" 'What then will this child become?'
For, indeed, the hand of the Lord was with him."

Take a few minutes to savor a word, a phrase, a question, or a feeling that rises up in you. Reflect on this quietly or share it aloud.

The other Scripture readings of the day are

Isaiah 49:1-6

Psalm 139:1-3

Acts of the Apostles 13:22-26

Invitation to Reflect on the Gospel

Part of the fun of encountering a baby is guessing what the child will be in adult life.

"Look at the size of those hands! He's going to be a catcher!"

"Look at the length of her fingers! She's going to be a pianist!"

Of course, our speculation is based on superficial signs and is purely whimsical. If we're right about the child's future, it's a coincidence. However, in the case of John the Baptist, whose birth we observe on this date each year, the adults around him had more than superficial reasons to wonder what this baby would do with his life.

One reason was that the birth of John was foretold to his father, Zachariah, by the archangel Gabriel (Luke 1:13). Another reason was that John's mother, Elizabeth, was childless and well beyond the age for childbirth. Still another reason was that, as today's Gospel reading recalls, Gabriel had taken away Zachariah's ability to speak after Zachariah refused to believe the angel (Luke 1:20) and restored it only after Zachariah gave the unborn child the name the angel had prescribed. No wonder people asked, "What, then, will this child become?"

The only person who could answer that question, in the fullness of time, was John himself.

The angel told Zachariah that the child would be "filled with the holy Spirit even from his mother's womb" (Luke 1:15), and some authorities, including St. Thomas Aquinas, have believed that means John was cleansed of original sin while in his mother's womb (cf. Thomas Aquinas, *Summa Theologica*, q. 27, a. 6). Certainly, when he had been born and "grew and became strong in spirit," John discerned God's will—what God wanted him to do. John understood that God wanted him to call on people to re-form their lives, to live with each other in a relationship of social and economic justice, and to prepare for the immanent coming of the messiah, the judge and savior of the world.

This was not a simple vocation. By deciding to undertake it, John was deciding to forgo any occupation that might have provided him with common food, clothing, and housing. He was deciding to forgo any chance at status and privilege. Moreover, he was deciding to confront people who were comfortable in their positions of wealth and power, people who were not accustomed to looking honestly at their lives and their relationships. He was deciding to make himself the target of what turned out to be a lethal antagonism.

This was the future John accepted when he accepted the will of God.

Invitation to Group Sharing

1. When have you rejoiced with a relative, friend, or neighbor who has benefited from some good fortune? How hard or easy is it to share another's joy without envy?

2. We are familiar with scriptural stories such as the conception and birth of John the Baptist, but do we truly believe that God is at work in the lives of people in our own time – for that matter, in our own lives? Share insights.

3. How have you responded when you have felt God calling you to do something that might disrupt the usual order of your life? How will you respond as a result of our sharing about John the Baptist?

Invitation to Act

Determine a specific action (individual or group) that flows from your sharing. This should be your primary consideration. When choosing an individual action, determine what you will do and share it with the group. When choosing a group action, determine who will take responsibility for different aspects of the action. The following are secondary suggestions:

1. Reflect prayerfully and make a list of people or situations in your life that could weaken your faith in God's promises. Decide on a step you can step to counteract these influences.

2. Take a prayerful survey of your daily routine and pick one thing that could adjusted to allow you a few moments "in the wilderness" of solitude and quiet where you can be alone with God.

3. Decide on a concrete action through which you can acknowledge Christ before others.

Invitation to Closing Prayer

Give thanks to God, aloud or silently, for insights gained, for desires awakened, for directions clarified, for the gift of one another's openness and sensitivity. Conclude with the following, reciting it aloud.

Leader: Almighty God, you blessed Elizabeth and Zechariah by giving them the privilege of nurturing not only a son but the prophet who would announce the coming of the Lamb of God.

All: **Help us to continue answering John's call to make straight the way of the Lord by removing from our lives any obstacles to complete faith in your Son and compliance with your will.**

Leader: We ask this through our Lord Jesus Christ who lives and reigns with you and the Holy Spirit, world without end.

All: **Amen.**

SOLEMNITY OF SAINT PETER AND SAINT PAUL

June 29

"Who do you say I am"

Invitation to Pray

Pause for a few moments of silence to enter more deeply into the presence of God.

Song

Only this I want

Proclaim the Gospel

Matthew 16:13-19

"And I tell you, you are Peter. . . . I will give you the keys of the kingdom of heaven. . . ."

Take a few minutes to savor a word, a phrase, a question, or a feeling that rises up in you. Reflect on this quietly or share it aloud.

The other Scripture readings of the day are

Acts of the Apostles 12:1-11

Psalm 33:2-9

2 Timothy 4:6-8, 17-18

Invitation to Reflect on the Gospel

Have you ever watched a ceremony televised from the square outside the Vatican Basilica in Rome? During quiet moments in ceremonies, when not too much is happening, the camera often focuses on two giant statues nears the stairs leading up to the basilica doors They represent St. Peter, holding keys, and St. Paul, holding a letter in his left hand and a sword in his right.

Today the Church invites us to celebrate these two foundational figures, with passages from Scripture that focus on Peter and Paul. However, they are only the primary focus, because through them, the Scriptures are also inviting us to consider the essential features of what it means to be a follower of Christ today.

That is nowhere clearer than in today's Gospel. Jesus starts with the question, "Who do people say that the Son of Man is?" The answers he gets are extremely complimentary, recognizing him as the equivalent of a great prophet. When Jesus asks the disciples directly, "Who do you say that I am?" it is Peter who speaks up on behalf of them all, recognizing Jesus as the Christ, and as the Son of the living God. Jesus then makes the promise that probably all of us can recite by heart: "You are Peter, and on this rock I will build my church ... I will give you the keys of the kingdom of heaven. . . ."

Part of the depth of today's Gospel lies not just in the answer Peter gives, but in the fact that Jesus asks two very different questions. If he were asking us today, his first question might be,

"What did Peter and Paul say about me?" Let's hope we could give very good answers. But today, as on that day long ago in Caesarea Philippi, the Lord's bigger question is "Who do *you* say I am?"

The other important part of today's feast is that for both Peter and Paul, what they "said" about Jesus in their words or letters was matched by what they "said" by their actions, how they lived their lives, to the extent that both were martyred for acclaiming Jesus as the Son of the living God. Following Jesus comes at a price: the first reading starts with Peter under arrest; the second reading is written by Paul as a prisoner in Rome. Yet both readings are filled with a confidence in God: in the first reading, Peter attributes his escape to God; Paul, sensing that his execution is imminent, writes of God bringing him safe to greater, spiritual rescue.

We who can buy and use copies of PrayerTime do not live in a culture in which we are likely to suffer outright martyrdom for our beliefs, but there are so many little ways that today's culture can kill off our spiritual or faith life. We don't find many popular preachers today who warn us that being a Christian is a struggle. The Gospel is realistic about the struggle. However, the Gospel is always mindful of our human nature, and one way in which that is expressed is in the lives of the two saints we celebrate today. Scripture does not sanitize their stories, but shows us that there was another side. Paul, remember, was a fanatical persecutor of the Church. Moments after the promise we hear in today's Gospel, Jesus has to reprimand Peter for completely misunderstanding (verses 21-23). The glorious moment of Peter walking on the water suddenly becomes a moment of sinking doubt. Yes, there is Peter's magnificent triple declaration, after the resurrection, that he loves Jesus; but there is that awful earlier moment when Peter denies Christ three times. The Gospel does not demand the impossible; it simply demands the possible, well done. The Gospel does not deny we may get things wrong; it asks us not to deny it, and to get it right from then on.

Too difficult, some say, and that's another reason to look to Peter and Paul. Underlying all they achieved there is a fundamental conviction that we are invited to share. Paul always acknowledges that he is what he is by the grace of God. And in today's Gospel, when Jesus compliments Peter for giving such a good answer to his question, Jesus signals that this, too, is by the grace of God: "flesh and blood has not revealed this to you, but my Father in heaven." Baptism is a call to follow Jesus, but it is entrusts us to the Spirit who strengthens us to live up to this high calling.

There are so many points of similarity between Peter and Paul; yet we know that they had their differences. One of the great turning points in the history of the Church came because Paul felt that his call from God to be apostle to the non-Jews obliged him to challenge Peter, who until then saw the apostolate as being only to Jews. Both were deeply committed to the single mission of Christ, yet they agreed that difference is part of how that mission is carried out.

Next time we see St. Peter's Square, full of people, being televised, perhaps we can watch out for those two statues and remember: one Church, many people; one mission, many ministries. That's what "Catholic" really means. What are we doing to make it come true?

Invitation to Group Sharing

1. What do you find inspiring in the lives of Peter and Paul? What do you find comforting in the lives of Peter and Paul?

2. Share with the group what the word "Catholic" is taken to mean, and what you think it really should mean.

3. In one sentence, how would you express your faith in Jesus? What does your faith in Jesus mean in terms of how you live?

Invitation to Act

Determine a specific action (individual or group) that flows from your sharing. This should be your primary consideration.

When choosing an individual action, determine what you will do and share it with the group. When choosing a group action, determine who will take responsibility for different aspects of the action. The following are secondary suggestions:

1. Paul dared to go beyond the first community of converts from Judaism, to take the Gospel to the Gentiles. Think of a way to reach out to those who are not in the local parish community.

2. Find out about areas of the world where people are persecuted for their Christian faith, and if there are ways you can help, either individually, or as group within the parish.

3. Find the Second Letter to Timothy, and read it prayerfully and slowly. Think of this as Paul's last message. Journal the thoughts that this message prompts.

Invitation to Closing Prayer

Give thanks to God, aloud or silently, for the faith entrusted to us by all those who have gone before us, especially the apostles Peter and Paul. Give thanks for their witness, and for the freedom we have to gather in small communities to faith share.

Conclude with the following prayer:

**Father, Lord and Giver of Life,
we turn to you in faith and proclaim
that Jesus is the Christ, your only-begotten Son.
Fill us with the desire to live out what we profess.
Send us your Spirit to give us the strength**

and courage we need,
so that our lives may be for your glory,
and for the salvation of the world.
This we ask through Christ our Lord.
Amen.

FEAST OF THE TRANSFIGURATION

August 6

"Listen to Him"

Invitation to Pray

Pause for a few moments of silence to enter more deeply into the presence of God.

Song

Gather Us In

Proclaim the Gospel

Year A: Matthew 17:1-9

Year B: Mark 9:2-10

Year C: Luke 9:28b-36

The Transfiguration

" A cloud cast a shadow over them."

Take a few minutes to savor a word, a phrase, a question, or a feeling that rises up in you. Reflect on this quietly or share it aloud.

The other Scripture readings of the day are

Daniel 7:9-10, 13-14
Psalm 97:1-2, 5-5, 9 (1a, 9a)
2 Peter 1:16-19

Invitation to Reflect on the Gospel

The contrast between light and darkness is a frequent motif in the Scriptures, and it plays an important part in the accounts of the Transfiguration in the Gospels of Matthew, Mark, and Luke. In this mystical episode, light—

a brilliant, white light—is a sign of the divinity of Jesus. The three apostles, who saw Jesus not only bathed in this light but emitting it from his own person, were getting a privileged glimpse of the Reality—the presence of God in the world here and now—that transcends the usual experiences of human life.

Moreover, Peter, James, and John could see in this shimmering tableau the images of Moses and Elijah who had been faithful to God, who had served God's people, and who, through the sacrifice of Jesus, would live in the glow of God's presence—a promise the apostles might apply to themselves.

No wonder Peter did not want that light to be dimmed, did not want that moment to end. But it did end, and it ended in the darkness of a gathering cloud.

The apostles who accompanied Jesus to what many believe was the summit of Mount Tabor had a unique experience, but Pope Benedict XVI suggested in a homily that we all may experience something similar in substance if not in intensity: "a momentary foretaste of what will constitute the happiness of Paradise.... usually brief experiences that are sometimes granted by God, especially prior to difficult trials."

This insight, this intuition, this awareness may occur during prayer, during liturgy, during reading and contemplation, during an exercise of charity or compassion.

But, the pope said, no one can spend his whole earthly life on Tabor.

"Indeed," he said "human existence is a journey of faith and as such, moves ahead more in shadows than in full light, and is no stranger to moments of obscurity and also of complete darkness."

How reassuring it would be if we could "see" God every day as the apostles saw him in the blazing light on Tabor, but Pope Benedict reminded us that in this life our relationship with God is a matter of listening, not of seeing. Our path in this life is illuminated by "the interior light that is kindled in us by the Word of God."

For an example, the pope turned in his homily to Mary, who was closest to God among all human beings and yet "still had to walk day after day in a pilgrimage of faith," constantly meditating on God's word in Scripture and on the events in the life of her son, Jesus.

It is Mary who first told us regarding her son, "Listen to him," the words that would be spoken by the Father during the epiphany on the mountaintop.

This, Pope Benedict said, "is the gift and duty for each one of us. ... to listen to Christ, like Mary. To listen to him in his Word, contained in Sacred Scripture. To listen to him in the events of our lives, seeking to decipher in them the messages of Providence. Finally, to listen to him in our brothers and sisters, especially in the lowly and the poor, to whom Jesus himself demands our concrete love. To listen to Christ and obey his voice: this is the principal way, the only way, that leads to the fullness of joy and of love" (Pope Benedict XVI, *Angelus*, March 12, 2006).

Invitation to Group Sharing

1. When have you experienced "a foretaste of what will constitute the happiness of Paradise"?

2. What has helped you maintain your faith in God's promises during the dark times in your life?

3. In what ways do you respond to the Father's command regarding his Son: "Listen to him"?

Invitation to Act

Determine a specific action (individual or group) that flows from your sharing. This should be your primary consideration. When choosing an individual action, determine what you will do and share it with the group. When choosing a group action, determine who will take responsibility for different aspects of the action. The following are secondary suggestions:

1. Review your daily routine and determine where you can add even a little stillness and silence to your life and then use that quiet time each day to listen to God.

2. As one way of listening to Jesus, join a Bible study group in your parish. If your parish has no such group, help to start one.

3. Consider who in your parish community may have difficulty hearing the word of God. Consider those who are sight or hearing impaired, those whose first language is not spoken in your church, those who are homebound. Discuss with members of your group how you could help bring the word to at least one such person.

Invitation to Closing Prayer

Give thanks to God, aloud or silently, for insights gained, for desires awakened, for directions clarified, for the gift of one another's openness and sensitivity. Conclude with the following:

All: **O God, you revealed yourself in the birth, life and death, and resurrection of your Son, Jesus Christ.**
Although we cannot see you, we believe that you are near in the bright days and the dark days of our lives.
Help us to listen attentively to the Gospel and live each day in keeping with your word so that one day we might live in the light of your presence, world without end. Amen.

SOLEMNITY OF THE ASSUMPTION OF THE BLESSED VIRGIN MARY

August 15

All Generations Call Her Blessed

Invitation to Pray

Pause for a few moments of silence to enter more deeply into the presence of God.

Song

Hail Mary, Gentle Woman

Proclaim the Gospel

Luke 1:39-56

"The Almighty has done great things for me."

Take a few minutes to savor a word, a phrase, a question, or a feeling that rises up in you. Reflect on this quietly or share it aloud.

The other Scripture readings of the day are

Revelation 11:19a; 12:1-6a, 10 ab
Psalm 45:10, 11, 12, 16 (10bc)
1 Corinthians 15:20-27

Invitation to Reflect on the Gospel

Visitors to the Basilica of St. Peter in Rome enter through a massive portico that is embellished with statues, coats of arms, and inscriptions commemorating persons and events that were significant in the history of the Catholic Church.

Among the accoutrements in the portico is a plaque on which are listed the names of the cardinals and other bishops who attended the ceremony on November 1, 1950, at which Pope Pius XII promulgated the doctrine of the Assumption of the Blessed Virgin Mary.

By making this formal declaration, the pope was not adding something to traditional Catholic belief. On the contrary, Pius XII was defining as dogma something that Catholics had believed for more than sixteen centuries—namely that Mary, the mother of Jesus, was assumed bodily into heaven.

The names on the plaque at St. Peter's, the names of bishops from all over the world, symbolize how widely this belief was held. For many years, the Holy See had received petitions from individuals and organizations, from lay people and clergy, to declare the Assumption an article of faith for Catholics. Pius surveyed the bishops of his time as to whether this should be done, and he received nearly unanimous agreement.

The pope's pronouncement, which left open the question of whether Mary had died before the Assumption, linked this mystery to another: "She, by an entirely unique privilege, completely overcame sin by her Immaculate Conception, and as a result she was not subject to the law of remaining in the corruption of the grave, and she did not have to wait until the end of time for the redemption of her body" (Pope Pius XII, *Munificentissimus Deus*, §5).

In the document in which he announced this doctrine, the pope said he hoped Catholics would be inspired to a stronger piety toward Mary and that they "may be more and more convinced of the value of a human life entirely devoted to carrying out the heavenly Father's will and to bring good to others" (*Munificentissimus Deus*, §42).

His reference to "the value of human life" reminds us that Mary, despite the gift of her Immaculate Conception, was a human being like us. She was subject to all the labor, worry, fear, and frustration that human existence implies, including the particular burdens of a poor mother in first century Palestine whose son was often the object of rejection and ridicule and was ultimately the victim of an unjust and violent death. And yet Mary remained faithful to the commitment she made to God's will before her son was born.

The Assumption of her body into heaven renews the promise God made to each of us through Jesus—that we, too, can live forever in the presence of God and his saints if we are faithful to the commandments, loving God and each other.

"(W)hile the illusory teachings of materialism and the corruption of morals that follows from these teachings threaten to extinguish the light of virtue" and to ruin people's lives "by exciting discord among them," the pope wrote, "in this magnificent way all may see clearly to what a lofty goal our bodies and souls are destined. ... (I)t is our hope that belief in Mary's bodily Assumption into heaven will make our belief in our own resurrection stronger and render it more effective."

Invitation to Group Sharing

1. In what ways do you think of Mary as sharing your experience as a human being?

2. How does Mary's example help you to accept God's will and apply it to your life?

3. When has your hope of your own resurrection helped you to deal with life's pressures and problems?

Invitation to Act

Determine a specific action (individual or group) that flows from your sharing. This should be your primary consideration. When choosing an individual action, determine what you will do and share it with the group. When choosing a group action, determine who will take responsibility for different aspects of the action. The following are secondary suggestions:

1. Set aside a half hour each week in which you can regularly pray the rosary—alone, with your family, or with friends. Pray either the Joyful Mysteries of the Presentation or the Finding of the Child Jesus in the Temple, or the Luminous Mystery of the Wedding Feast at Cana, contemplating the ways in which Mary was a faithful witness to the ministry of Jesus. Or pray the Glorious Mysteries of the Assumption or the Crowning of Mary as Queen of Heaven, contemplating Mary's glorification as a sign of the promise Jesus made of eternal life for those who believe in him.

2. Determine whether there are any regular devotions to Mary, such as a novena or a communal rosary, in your parish. If there are, consider participating. If there are not, offer to research and organize one and perhaps lead it yourself.

3. The Assumption of Mary is inextricably connected to the promise of the resurrection of our own bodies. Consider organizing a ministry dedicated to Mary in which members of your parish attend vigil services and funerals for parishioners as a sign of hope to bereaved families and friends.

Invitation to Closing Prayer

Give thanks to God, aloud or silently, for insights gained, for desires awakened, for directions clarified, for the gift of one another's openness and sensitivity. Conclude with the following:

Almighty God,
you chose the Virgin Mary
to be both the instrument through whom
your Son was born into the world
and the first of his disciples.
May we follow her example
by remaining faithful to his gospel
in every aspect of our lives.
We ask this through your Son, Jesus Christ,
who lives and reigns with you
in the unity of the Holy Spirit,
one God, forever and ever. Amen.

FEAST OF THE TRIUMPH OF THE HOLY CROSS

September 14

"So must the Son of Man be lifted up"

Invitation to Pray

Pause for a few moments of silence to enter more deeply into the presence of God.

Song

Now We Remain

Proclaim the Gospel

John 3:13-17
The Son of Man Lifted Up

"For God so loved the world that he gave his only Son"

Take a few minutes to savor a word, a phrase, a question, or a feeling that rises up in you. Reflect on this quietly or share it aloud.

The other Scripture readings of the day are

Numbers 21:4b-9
Psalm 78:1-2, 34-35, 36-37, 38
Philippians 2:6-11

Invitation to Reflect on the Gospel

The feast we celebrate today is connected to the history of the Basilica of the Holy Sepulcher in Jerusalem, a church that reputedly was erected over the sites where Jesus was crucified and was buried.

According to tradition in which fact and legend are difficult to distinguish, the Emperor Constantine in the fourth century asked his mother, now known to us as St. Helena, to travel to the Holy Land to identify the important places in the life, death, and resurrection of Jesus.

One account has it that at Helena's direction, the cross on which Jesus was executed was unearthed and that it was placed in a church built on the spot at the direction of Constantine.

The church was consecrated on September 13, AD 335, and on September 14, as part of the celebration, the cross was carried outside for the people to venerate.

There are divergent stories about what became of the cross; many fragments of wood, scattered around the world, are said to be true relics.

Inasmuch as the cross was used by the Romans to inflict torture and death—to put an end to life—it may seem contradictory at first to speak of the "triumph" of the cross.

But, as Pope John Paul II explained, the Son of Man was "lifted up" on the cross not only to give up his life but to make possible eternal life for all who believed in him and in the Paschal mystery of which Calvary was an intrinsic chapter.

Speaking to Nicodemus who, as the pope pointed out, could not have anticipated the crucifixion, Jesus used an image that the scholarly Nicodemus would recognize— the image of the serpent lifted up by Moses in the desert.

We read in the Book of Numbers that as part of God's testing of Israel, he caused the people to be bitten by snakes, and God instructed Moses to hold up a brazen serpent so that those who looked on it would be healed.

People lived, John Paul said, not because they saw the serpent but because they believed in God's saving power.

In a similar way, all who look up at Jesus on the cross are saved because they believe in his power over sin and death.

"The analogy becomes even more striking," the pope said, "if we keep in mind that the salvation from physical death, caused by the poison of the serpents in the desert, came about through a serpent. *Salvation from spiritual death*—a death that was sin and was caused by man—*came about through a man*, through the Son of Man 'lifted up' " on the cross (Pope John Paul II, *Homily*, Arizona State University, September 14, 1987).

On the cross, we see the full measure of God emptying himself, as St. Paul put it (*Phil. 2:6-11*), experiencing human nature to the extreme of violent death, because God "so loved the world" that he willed for all people the triumph of resurrection.

Invitation to Group Sharing

1. What thoughts are stirred in you when you see Jesus on the cross?

2. Jesus said that anyone who wishes to be his disciple must "take up" the cross. What form has that cross taken in your life?

3. What people of what experiences have helped you to see beyond the death of the cross to the new life of resurrection?

Invitation to Act

Determine a specific action (individual or group) that flows from your sharing. This should be your primary consideration. When choosing an individual action, determine what you will do and share it with the group. When choosing a group action, determine who will take responsibility for different aspects of the action. The following are secondary suggestions:

1. Read one of the Gospel accounts of the crucifixion and prayerfully meditate on the temporary nature of the suffering we undergo in this life and the eternal nature of the new life God has promised those who love him.

2. If you don't wear a crucifix or display one in your home, consider doing so as a witness to your faith in the cross as the "gateway" to resurrection.

3. Visit, call, or write to someone who is seriously ill; prayerfully help that person focus on the resurrection that Jesus won for us by enduring the suffering of the cross.

Invitation to Closing Prayer

Give thanks to God, aloud or silently, for insights gained, for desires awakened, for directions clarified, for the gift of one another's openness and sensitivity. Conclude with the following:

Leader: Lord, Jesus Christ, you willingly gave your life on the cross as atonement for the sins of all humanity. Because of your sacrifice, death need not be the end for us. Like the cross itself, death can be the gateway to life forever with you, in the company of the Creator and the Holy Spirit.

All: **Lord Jesus, you said that those who would be your disciples must take up their cross and follow you. As we contemplate the cross on which you gave** your life, may we be even more encouraged not only to patiently bear the burdens of everyday life, but to enthusiastically seek to ease the burdens of the poor, the sick, and the neglected whom you love so much. By sharing with you the weight of the cross may we also share with you the triumph of resurrection. Amen.

SOLEMNITY OF ALL SAINTS

November 1

Theirs is the Kingdom of Heaven

Invitation to Pray

Pause for a few moments of silence to enter more deeply into the presence of God.

Song

> For All the Saints

Proclaim the Gospel

> *Matthew 5:1-12a*

> "Rejoice and be glad. Your reward will be great in heaven."

> *Take a few minutes to savor a word, a phrase, a question, or a feeling that rises up in you. Reflect on this quietly or share it aloud.*

> The other Scripture readings of the day are
>
> *Revelation 7:2-4, 9-14*
> *Psalm 24:1-2, 3-4, 5-6*
> *1 John 3:1-3*

Invitation to Reflect on the Gospel

St. Bernard of Clairvaux, the twelfth century abbot and reformer, asked a blunt and perhaps unexpected question about the solemnity we celebrate today. "Why," St. Bernard said in a homily on this date, "should our praise and glorification, or even the celebration of this feast day mean anything to the saints? What do they care about earthly honors when their heavenly Father honors them by fulfilling the faithful promise of the Son? What does our commendation mean to them? The saints have no need of honor from us; neither does our devotion add the slightest thing to what is theirs. Clearly, if we venerate their memory, it serves us, not them."

How does it serve us to venerate the memory of the saints—those formally recognized by the Church and those whose names we do not know?

St. Bernard answered that by saying that when he thought of the saints, he felt "inflamed by a tremendous yearning. ... to enjoy their company" (*Disc. 2, Opera Omnia Cisterc.* 5, 364ff).

So, as Pope Benedict XVI has pointed out, the meaning of today's observance is that we do not simply honor the saints in a passive way but look at their example and apply it to ourselves. We contemplate the lives of those who are "blessed" because they lived in keeping with the Gospel and, in particular, the Beatitudes, the call to humility, simplicity, mercy, charity, and faithfulness. And, the pope said, their example reawakens in us "the great longing to be like them: happy to live near God, in his light, in the great family of God's friends" (Pope Benedict XVI, *Homily at Holy Mass on the Solemnity of All Saints*, November 1, 2006).

In other words, when we pause to consider the lives of the saints, it inspires us to long for holiness in our own lives, and the path to holiness, Pope Benedict said, "always passes through the Way of the Cross." St. Bernard, again coming right to the point, addressed this with his contemporaries: "The saints want us to be with them, and we are indifferent. The souls of the just await us, and we ignore them. Come... let us at length spur ourselves on. We must rise again with

Christ; we must seek the world that is above and set our mind on the things of heaven."

This does not come as a surprise to us; Jesus told us those who want to follow him must deny themselves and take up the cross, meaning that they must imitate him and live in keeping with his Gospel day to day, at home, at school, at work, in the community. They bend their will to his, they honor and glorify him, and they live as he did by making the needs and cares of others as important as their own.

To the extent that we set out each day, each one in his or her own circumstances, to follow Jesus, Pope Benedict said, "we too can participate in his blessedness. With him, the impossible becomes possible, and even a camel can pass through the eye of a needle" (cf. Mt. 19:24-26).

Invitation to Group Sharing

1. Who is a saint that you particularly admire, and how has that person's example affected you?

2. Pope Benedict said the path to holiness leads through the Way of the Cross. How might you apply that to your own life? What cross do you or can you take up in order to strive for holiness?

3. Although the saints are in heaven, what experiences have made you feel close to them?

Invitation to Act

Determine a specific action (individual or group) that flows from your sharing. This should be your primary consideration. When choosing an individual action, determine what you will do and share it with the group. When choosing a group action, determine who will take responsibility for different aspects of the action. The following are secondary suggestions:

1. Read the Beatitudes carefully and prayerfully, and consider how each of them might apply to your life today.

2. Consult a Catholic calendar at the beginning of each month and take note of the saints to be honored at daily Masses. Select one or two saints with whom you are not familiar and research their lives to learn about the example they set. Make a point of remembering those saints on their feast days.

3. If your parish is named for a saint, what provisions have been made to make parishioners, including children, familiar with their patron? Consider how you, alone or with your group, can assist in this area—for example, by researching the saint's life and producing a brochure to distribute to current and new parishioners, or by working with the liturgical team to establish a devotion to the saint, perhaps coupled with a fellowship event, on his or her feast day.

Invitation to Closing Prayer

Give thanks to God (aloud or silently) for insights gained, for desires awakened, for directions clarified, for the gift of one another's openness and sensitivity. Conclude with the following brief litany of the saints. (The leader may ask members of the group to take turns leading this prayer.)

Reader 1:   Lord, have mercy on us.

All: **Christ, have mercy on us.**

Reader 1:   Lord, have mercy on us.

All: **Christ, hear us.**

Reader 2:   God, the Father of heaven

All: **Have mercy on us.**

Reader 2:   God, the Son, Redeemer of the world

All: **Have mercy on us.**

Reader 2:   God, the Holy Spirit

All: **Have mercy on us.**

Reader 2:   Holy Trinity, one God

All: **Have mercy on us.**

Reader 3:   Holy Mary

All: **Pray for us.**

Reader 3:   Mother of Jesus

All: **Pray for us.**

Reader 3:   Queen of Heaven

All: **Pray for us.**

Reader 4:   St. Michael the Archangel

All: **Pray for us.**

Reader 4:   St. Gabriel

All: **Pray for us.**

Reader 4:   All you Holy Angels and Archangels

All: **Pray for us.**

Reader 5:   St. John the Baptist

All: **Pray for us.**

Reader 5:   St. Joseph

All: **Pray for us.**

Reader 5:   All you Holy Patriarchs and Prophets

All: **Pray for us.**

Reader 6:   St. Peter

All: **Pray for us.**

Reader 6:   St. Paul

All: **Pray for us.**

Reader 6:   St. Matthew

All: **Pray for us.**

Reader 6:   St. Mark

All: **Pray for us.**

Reader 6:   All you holy Apostles and Evangelists

All: **Pray for us.**

Leader: St. Francis of Assisi

All: **Pray for us.**

Leader: St. Mary Magdalene

All: **Pray for us.**

Leader: St. Catherine of Siena

All: **Pray for us.**

Leader: All you holy Saints of God

All: **Pray for us.**

All: **O God, as we contemplate the lives of your saints, may we be inspired to follow their example by keeping your commandments and by living lives of compassion and charity for those who most need our help.**

     We ask this through Jesus Christ, our Lord, who lives and reigns with you and the Holy Spirit, one God, for ever and ever. Amen.

THE COMMEMORATION OF ALL THE FAITHFUL DEPARTED
(ALL SOULS DAY)

November 2

"The Souls of the Just are in the Hand of God" – Wisdom 3:1

Invitation to Pray

Pause for a few moments of silence to enter more deeply into the presence of God.

Song
We Shall Rise Again

Proclaim the Gospel

Matthew 5:1-12a*

"Blessed are the clean of heart,

for they will see God"

Take a few minutes to savor a word, a phrase, a question, or a feeling that rises up in you. Reflect on this quietly or share it aloud.

The other Scripture readings of the day are

Wisdom 3:1-9

Psalm 23:1-3a, 3b-4, 5, 6 (1) (4ab)

Romans 5:5-11

---

*   The Church has authorized numerous options for all of the readings during celebration of the Eucharist on this day. Consult the *Lectionary for Mass* for optional readings not listed here.

Invitation to Reflect on the Gospel

One of the best known works of art in the world is *The Last Judgment*, the colossal fresco created in the sixteenth century by Michelangelo Buonarroti on the wall behind the altar of the Sistine Chapel in Rome. The painting is dominated by an image of the risen Jesus with his right arm raised in condemnation of the souls being taken to hell, depicted in the lower right hand corner of the scene.

It is a grim picture and one that might easily inspire fear of death and despair for those who have died. But Michelangelo also included in this fresco figures of the souls who are not condemned, those who had served the Lord by serving the least of his brothers and sisters, those whom Jesus had already welcomed to eternal life in the presence of God (cf. Matthew 25:31-46). These figures, the figures of the saved, represent the hope that is the focus of this annual observance, All Souls Day.

In his first letter to the Church in Thessalonica, St. Paul urged Christians not to grieve over the dead "like the rest who have no hope. For if we believe that Jesus died and rose, so too will God, through Jesus, bring with him those who have fallen asleep" (1 Thessalonians 4:13b-14). Citing this passage, Pope Benedict XVI found All Souls Day to be a particularly good occasion for us "to renew the hope in eternal life, founded on Christ's death and resurrection" (*Angelus*, November 2, 2008). The Church embraces and even celebrates this hope; the first prayer in the vigil service for the dead begins by invoking "the God of hope."

Nor is there any reason to limit our hope. Pope John Paul II, in a letter marking the millennium of All Souls Day, pointed out that while the Church is necessary to salvation, the mercy of God embraces all people: "Those indeed who are in ignorance of Christ's Gospel and of his

Church through no fault of their own, who search for God in sincerity of heart, and who, acting according to conscience, strive under the influence of grace to fulfill his will, belong to his people, even though in a way we cannot see, and can obtain eternal salvation. Their number is known only to God" (Letter to Most Rev. Raymond Segûy, abbot of Cluny, June 2, 1998, citing Paul VI, *Credo of the People of God*, June 1968).

Pope Benedict also reminded us that this hope is not only individual and self-centered. "Our lives are profoundly linked, one to the other," the pope has said, "and the good and bad that each of us does always affects others too." This idea is stressed in the vigil prayers which declare our belief "that all the ties of friendship and affection which have knit us as one throughout our lives do not unravel with death."

We do not, therefore, yearn for and pray for eternal life only for ourselves with no reference to others; the Church urges us to pray for those who have died and whose souls are in Purgatory awaiting the beatific vision—our relatives and friends, but also those whom we have never known. We do this during the celebration of Mass in which the Eucharistic prayer and the general intercessions include prayers for the dead; we are encouraged to do it whenever we pray.

"The prayers of intercession and petition which the Church never ceases to raise to God have great value. ..." Pope John Paul wrote. "The Lord always lets himself be moved by his children's supplications, for he is the God of the living. ..." When we entrust to the Lord the souls who have died, the pope wrote, "we recognize our solidarity with them and share in their salvation in this wondrous mystery of the communion of saints."

Invitation to Group Sharing

1. When you experience the death of a friend or loved one, what helps you deal with your grief and sense of loss?

2. What helps you feel connected to relatives and friends who have died?

3. What gives you hope when you contemplate your own death?

Invitation to Act

Determine a specific action (individual or group) that flows from your sharing. This should be your primary consideration. When choosing an individual action, determine what you will do and share it with the group. When choosing a group action, determine who will take responsibility for different aspects of the action. The following are secondary suggestions:

1. Consider establishing a ministry that assures that some members of the parish demonstrate hope and solidarity by attending vigil services and funerals for the relatives and friends of your fellow parishioners.

2. Consider establishing a ministry that offers to provide transportation and other assistance to elderly or disabled parishioners who wish to visit a cemetery in your area to pray for their deceased loved ones.

3. Consider establishing a ministry committed to pray for the souls of deceased parishioners on the anniversaries of their deaths and notifying their families by sending a prayer card.

Invitation to Closing Prayer

Give thanks to God, aloud or silently, for insights gained, for desires awakened, for directions clarified,

*for the gift of one another's openness and sensitivity.
Conclude with the following:*

All: **Lord Jesus Christ,
the Father sent you into the world
not to condemn it, but that it might be saved.
Look with mercy on those who have died
after striving in their lives to do your will.
We pray that they may be welcomed,
as we too hope to be,
to live forever in the presence of the one God,
Father, Son, and Holy Spirit. Amen.**

FEAST OF THE DEDICATION OF THE BASILICA OF ST. JOHN LATERAN

November 9

"He was Speaking of the Temple of his Body"

Invitation to Pray

Pause for a few moments of silence to enter more deeply into the presence of God.

Song

All Are Welcome

Proclaim the Gospel

John 2:13-22

The Temple of his Body

"His disciples remembered that it was written, 'Zeal for your house will consume me.' "

Take a few minutes to savor a word, a phrase, a question, or a feeling that rises up in you. Reflect on this quietly or share it aloud.

The other Scripture readings of the day are

Ezekiel 47:1-2, 8-9, 12
Psalm 46:3, 4, 5-6, 8, 11 (5)
1 Corinthians 3:9c-11, 16-17

Invitation to Reflect on the Gospel

The word "zeal" doesn't come up very often in conversation.

Perhaps that's because "zeal" refers to a level of passion that itself is unusual—the level of passion Jesus demonstrated in the incident described in the passage from St. John's Gospel.

The Gospel tells us that when Jesus drove the merchants and money changers from the temple area his followers recalled a verse in Psalm 69, but the author of the Gospel did not quote the whole verse: "Because zeal for your house consumes me, I am scorned by those who scorn you" (Psalm 69:10).

The zeal that prompted Jesus to make such a bold gesture was not for the building itself—an elaborate structure that had enveloped the Second Temple built about 500 years before he was born. The temple of Jesus' time had been built by Herod the Great as part of a larger scheme to assure the king's lasting fame. But Jesus' zeal was for the temple as a sign of God's presence among his people and as a focal point for the people's worship of God and faithfulness to God's commandments.

As we hear already in this gospel passage, that zeal, far from being appreciated and respected, would be misinterpreted, distorted, and held against Jesus.

The Church brings this subject to our attention on a feast day devoted not to the Lord or one of the saints, as most solemnities and feast days are, but to the dedication in 324 AD of what is now the Basilica of St. John Lateran in Rome.

The full name of this glorious structure, which has been ruined and rebuilt over the ages, is "Archbasilica of the Most Holy Savior and Ss. John the Baptist and the Evangelist at the Lateran." An inscription between the main doors calls it "of all the churches in the city and the world, the mother and head."

Those titles refer to the fact that St. John Lateran, although it is outside the Vatican, is the cathedral church of the bishop of Rome—the pope—and, in that sense, the cathedral church for Catholics everywhere.

It is important not only as an historic artifact but as the prototype of every church where people gather because they *believe* that Jesus Christ—raised from the dead in the temple of his body— is actually present among them, as he promised he would be; where God is actually present as his word is proclaimed; where Jesus Christ is present in flesh and blood in the bread and wine of the Eucharist.

It is the fulfillment of Jesus' promise—"there am I in the midst of them"—that should fill us with zeal, with passion, for our encounter with the Lord, whether in St. John Lateran in Rome or in any church, grand or humble, anywhere in the world.Visitors to the Basilica of St. Peter in Rome enter through a massive portico that is embellished with statues, coats of arms, and inscriptions commemorating persons and events that were significant in the history of the Catholic Church.

Invitation to Group Sharing

1. What aspects of your parish church or of the liturgies you attend there most make you conscious of the real presence of God?

2. When have you experienced doubts or difficulties about the sacred character of your church or the liturgies celebrated there? How have you dealt with those doubts or difficulties?

3. How do you think your own participation in the ministries and the liturgies of the Church can help

other members of the assembly be more aware of God's real presence among them?

Invitation to Act

Determine a specific action (individual or group) that flows from your sharing. This should be your primary consideration. When choosing an individual action, determine what you will do and share it with the group. When choosing a group action, determine who will take responsibility for different aspects of the action. The following are secondary suggestions:

1. If you're accustomed to being in church mostly during liturgies, plan to regularly spend some time near the tabernacle when there are few or no distractions.

2. Inquire if your parish has a ministry that helps people who don't drive or don't own cars get to church. If it does, consider how you can help. If there is no such ministry, consider how you might help start one.

3. Inquire if your parish has a ministry that cares for very young children while their parents attend Mass. If it does, consider how you can help. If there is no such ministry, consider how you might help start one.

Invitation to Closing Prayer

Give thanks to God, aloud or silently, for being a real presence in your life. Alternatively, pray for faith that God is always near. Conclude with the following prayer, reciting it aloud:

Leader: Lord Jesus Christ, you promised that you would be present whenever we gather in your name.

All: **O Lord who is always by our side, help us to have faith in your pledge that you would not leave us orphaned; give us the perseverance to work through distractions, the fortitude to put aside doubts, and the**

fidelity to worship you in a world that believes only what it sees; keep us open to your presence in the sacraments, in your word, and in each other.

Leader: We ask this in your name, you who live with the Father and the Holy Spirit in the unity of the Trinity, one God, forever and ever.

All: **Amen.**

THE NATIVITY OF THE LORD

December 25

All Who Heard it were Amazed

Invitation to Pray

Pause for a few moments of silence to enter more deeply into the presence of God.

Song

Silent Night

Proclaim the Gospel

Luke 2:15-20*

"Mary kept all these things,
reflecting on them in her heart."

Take a few minutes to savor a word, a phrase, a question, or a feeling that rises up in you. Reflect on this quietly or share it aloud.

The other Scripture readings of the day are

Isaiah 62:11-12
Psalm 97:1,6,11-12
Titus 3:4-7

Invitation to Reflect on the Gospel

Considering the nature of the events in St. Luke's narrative of the birth of Jesus, we would expect from the witnesses exactly the reaction that Luke described:

---

*   The readings in this session are those designated for the Mass at Dawn. For the readings designated for the Mass at Midnight and the Mass during the Day, consult the *Lectionary for Mass.*

they were "amazed." But within the same few lines of Luke's story there is a tantalizing counterpoint to that amazement: "Mary kept all these things, reflecting on them in her heart." We have learned 20 centuries later about the birth of Jesus and all the circumstances surrounding it, and we hear the story repeated in a variety of ways scores of times during our lives. We have benefited from explanations of the Nativity, in homilies, in our religious instruction, in our reading. Do we, in the twenty-first century, have the same reactions to the birth of Jesus as those who were present at the time? Are we amazed, and do we reflect on these things in our hearts?

Although we are used to the story and all the images surrounding it—angels, shepherds, the manger, the parents, the infant—the meaning of these events should still amaze us. This is not a folk tale adorned with details calculated to charm us. This is the account of a transformative event in human history, an event in which divine life and human life intersected in a uniquely intimate way. This was God, so full of love for the creatures he made in his own likeness that he himself took on human form. This was God taking on himself the whole of the human experience, excepting sin, so that men and women would be restored to their proper relationship to God through the ministry, sacrifice, and glorification of Jesus, the man whose birth Luke described. If we believe this, how can we not be amazed?

As astounding as the birth of Jesus was in its implications for the human race, it was in its immediate circumstances a very personal event—this particular child born to these particular parents under difficult economic, social, and political conditions. Although it occurred in the first century in Palestine, a time and a place that are remote from us, we can easily relate to the story of Jesus' birth because we understand on the one hand fear and confusion, and we understand on the other hand the joy of parenthood and the irresistible attraction of a newborn child. For Joseph and Mary, the effects of these competing emotions must have been unsettling and exhausting. But Mary, as she often did, set an example for us in her reaction to the Nativity itself and the framework in which it occurred: she reflected on these things in her heart.

The Christmas season at times seems to be designed to prevent us from doing any such thing. The season imposes on us, and we impose on ourselves, so many material obligations—the season immerses us in so much activity and noise—that we may not pause to reflect on anything. But for most of us, the pressures of the holiday season are as nothing compared to what Mary confronted. And still, she reflected on these things in her heart. The birth of Jesus began the unfolding of the mystery through which each of us has been offered salvation from the consequences of sin and death. If we believe this, how can we not reflect on it at Christmas and on every day of our lives?

Invitation to Group Sharing

1. When have you seen an unexpected change in your life that you understood to be the result of God's will? How did you react to this change? What unexpected grace did you experience as a result?

2. What event or aspect of creation has made you feel amazement at the work of God?

3. When you think about Mary and Joseph as flesh-and-blood human beings experiencing the events Luke

describes in the Gospel, what are your reactions? How do you relate these events to your own life?

Invitation to Act

Determine a specific action (individual or group) that flows from your sharing. This should be your primary consideration. When choosing an individual action, determine what you will do and share it with the group. When choosing a group action, determine who will take responsibility for different aspects of the action. The following are secondary suggestions:

1. On several days during the year outside the Christmas season—perhaps in March, June, and September—prayerfully read Luke 1:26-35 and Matthew 1:18-21. Reflect on the readings with an awareness of what the angel was telling Mary and Joseph and awareness that the woman and man hearing this message were human beings like us. In the stillness of your prayer, be conscious of your own reaction to what God did at that moment in history.

2. Write a summary of what you did to prepare for the celebration of Christmas this year. Then draft a plan for how you would like to spend that time next year, focusing on the ways in which you would like to make the true meaning of the Nativity the focus of your preparation.

3. With your group, brainstorm ways in which your parish, during next Advent, can help its tweens and teens see beyond superficial images of Christmas and understand the birth of Jesus as a real event that happened to real people and as God's unique entry into human history. Outline a plan and recommend it to your pastor or faith-formation director.

Invitation to Closing Prayer

Give thanks to God (aloud or silently) for insights gained, for desires awakened, for directions clarified, for the gift of one another's openness and sensitivity. Conclude with the following:

Almighty God,

through the action of the Holy Spirit

you were born into human history

as the child Jesus, the son of Mary.

We celebrate the Nativity

with our hearts full of gratitude for this gift,

for the gift of the man Jesus grew to be,

and for the gift of eternal life,

won for us by his death and resurrection.

We make this prayer of thanks to you,

the one God—Father, Son, and Holy Spirit.

Amen.

MUSIC RESOURCES

Alphabetical Index of Suggested Songs
(by first line and/or title)

All Are Welcome
Words and Music: Marty Haugen
© 1994 GIA Publications, Inc.

Amazing Grace
Words: verses 1-4, John Newton
(1725-1807), verse 5, attributed to
John Rees
Music: traditional melody
Public domain

Be Not Afraid
Words (based on Isaiah 43:2-3
and Luke 6:2ff) and music:
Robert J. Dufford SJ
© 1975, 1978 Robert J. Dufford SJ
and OCP Publications

Bring Forth the Kingdom
Words and music: Marty Haugen
© 1986 GIA Publications, Inc.

**Come Back to Me with All
Your Heart**
see Hosea

Come, Holy Ghost, Creator Blest
Words: *Veni, Creator Spiritus*
attributed to Rabanus Maurus
(776-856), translated by Edward
Caswall (1814-1878)
Public domain

Come, Live in the Light
see We Are Called

Come to Me, All You Weary
see We shall rise again

Deep Within
Words (based on Jeremiah 31:33,
Ezekiel 36:26, and Joel 2:12) and
music: David Hass
© 1987 GIA Publications, Inc.

Do Not Fear to Hope
Words and music: Rory Cooney
© spiritandsong.com

Eye Has Not Seen
Words (based on 1 Corinthians
2:9-10) and music: Marty Haugen
© 1982 GIA Publications, Inc.

Gather Us In
Words and music: Marty Haugen
© 1982 GIA Publications, Inc.

God, Beyond All Names
Words and music: Bernadette
Farrell © 1990 Bernadette Farrell,
published by OCP Publications

God Has Chosen Me
Words and music: Bernadette
Farrell © 1990 Bernadette Farrell,
published by OCP Publications

God of Day and God of Darkness
Words and music: Marty Haugen
© 1985, 1994 GIA Publications

Hail Mary, Gentle Woman
Words (based on Luke 1:28) and
music: Carey Landry
© 1975, 1978 Carey Landry and
OCP Publications

Here I Am, Lord
Words (based on Isaiah 6) and
music: Dan Schutte
© 1981, 2003 OCP Publications

Hosea
Words (based on Hosea 6:1, 3:3, 2:16, 21, Joel 2:12) and music: Gregory Norbet, OSB
© 1972, 1980 The Benedictine Foundation of the State of Vermont, Inc.

How Beautiful on the Mountains
Words (based on Isaiah 52:7 and Matthew 4:17, 11:5, 28:18-20) and music: Lucien Deiss
© 1982 Lucien Deiss, published by OCP Publications

How Can I Keep from Singing?
Words and music: Robert Lowry (1826-1899)
Public domain

I Heard the Voice of Jesus Say
Words: Horatius Borar (1809-1889)
Music: Traditional, harmonized by Ralph Vaughan Williams (1872-1958)
Music © Oxford University Press

I Will Come to You in the Silence
see You Are Mine

In the Breaking of the Bread
Words: Bob Hurd and Michael Downey
Music: Bob Hurd
© 1989 OCP Publications

Isaiah 58
Words (based on Isaiah 58) and music: John Michael Talbot
© Birdwing Music/BMG Songs

Jesus, Come to Us
Words and music: David Hass
© 1981, 1982 OCP Publications

Joy to the World
Words (based on Psalm 98):
Isaac Watts (1674-1748)
Music: George F. Handel (1685-1759)
Public domain

Leaning on the Everlasting Arms
Words: Elisha A. Hoffman
Music: Anthony J. Showalter (1858-1924)
Public domain

Led by the Spirit
Words (based on Joel 2:12-13, Matthew 1:12-15, John 4:5-42):
Bob Hurd
© 1996 Bob Hurd, published by OCP Publications
Music: English traditional melody, adapted by Ralph Vaughan Williams (1872-1958)
© OUP

Lord of the Dance
Words and music: Sydney Carter (1915-2004)
©1963 Stainer and Bell Ltd., London

Lord, Who Throughout These Forty Days
Words: Claudia F. Hernaman (1838-1898)
Public domain

Lord, You Have Come
Words: Cesáreo Gabaráin; English translation: OCP
Music: Cesáreo Gabaráin
© 1979, 1987 Cesáreo Gabaráin, published by OCP Publications

Loving and Forgiving
Words (based on Psalm 103: 1-4, 8, 10-12) and music: Scott Soper
© 1992 Scott Soper, published by OCP Publications

Make me a channel of your peace
See Prayer of Saint Francis

Mine Eyes Have Seen the Glory
Words: Julia Howe
Music: Battle Hymn of the Republic
with refrain attributed to
William Steffe

My life flows on in endless song
see How can I keep from singing?

No Longer Strangers
see Isaiah 58

Now We Remain
Words (based on 1 Corinthians 1,
1 John, 2 Timothy) and music:
David Hass
© 1983 GIA Publications, Inc

O Come, O Come, Emmanuel
Words: *Veni, veni, Emmanuel*
translated by John M. Neale(1818-
1866)
Music: adapted from Gregorian
Mode I
Public domain

O Lord, Hear My Prayer
Words based on Psalm 102
Music: Jacques Berthier
© 1982 Les Presses de Taizé,
GIA Publications, Inc. agent

O Lord, our help in ages past
Words (based on Psalm 90):
Isaac Watts (1674-1784)
Music: attributed to William Croft
(1678-1727)
Public domain

On Holy Ground
Words and music: Donna Pena
©1992, 1994 GIA Publications, Inc.

On Jordan's Bank
Words: Charles Coffin(1676-1749),
translated by John Chandler
(1806-1876)
Public domain

One Bread, One Body
Words (based on 1 Corinthians
10:16-17, 12:4, 12-13, 21;
Galatians3:28; Ephesians 4:46; the
Didaché 9) and music: John Foley
SJ
© 1978, 1996, 2003 John Foley SJ
and OCP Publications

Only This I Want
Words based on Philippians 3:7-16,
2:15, 18
Music: Daniel L. Schutte
© 1981 Daniel L. Schutte and
OCP Publications

Out of Darkness
Words and Music: Christopher
Walker
© 1989 Christopher Walker,
published by OCO Publications

Peace, My Friends
Words and music: Ray Repp
© 1967 Otter Creek Music,
published by OCP Publications

Pie Jesu
Words: from the final verse of *Dies
Irae* (13th century) and the *Agnus
Dei* of the Requiem Mass
Public domain
Music: Andrew Lloyd-Weber
© 1985 The Really Useful Group Ltd
Original recording available on
Universal Records; Charlotte
Church recording on Sony/BMG
Records
Sheet music available from Hal
Leonard Publishing

Prayer of Saint Francis
Words (based on Prayer of St Francis of Assisi [1182-1226]) and music: Sebastian Temple (1928-1997)
© 1967, 2003 OCP Publications

Silent Night, Holy Night
Words: Joseph Mohr (1792-1849), translated by John F. Young (1820-1885)
Music: Franz X. Gruber (1787-1863)
Public domain

Sing of Mary, Meek and Lowly
Words: Roland Palmer and Omer Westendorf
Music: Richard Proulx
© 1986, GIA Publications, Inc.

Sing to the Mountains
Words (based on Psalm 118) and music: Robert J. Dufford SJ
© 1975, 1979 Robert J. Dufford and OCP Publications

Sing with All the Saints in Glory
Words (based on 1 Corinthians 15:20): William J. Irons (1812-1883)
Music: Ludwig van Beethoven (1770-1827)
Public domain

Song of the Body of Christ
Words and music: David Haas
© 1989 GIA Publications

That There May Be Bread
Words and music: Gregory Norbert
© 1979 The Benedictine Foundation of the State of Vermont, Inc.

The Cry of the Poor
Words (based on Psalm 34:2-3, 6-7, 18-19, 23) and music: John B. Foley SJ
© 1978, 1990 John B. Foley SJ and OCP Publications

The King of Love My Shepherd Is
Words (based on based on Psalm 23) and music: Henry William Baker (1821-1877)
Public domain

The Kingdom of God
Words: Bryn A. Rees (1911-1938);
© Mrs Olwen Scott
Music: Charles H. H. Parry (1848-1918); Public Domain

The Lord hears the cry of the poor
see The Cry of the Poor

They'll Know We Are Christians
Words and music: Peter Scholtes
© 1966 FEL Publications, assigned 1991 to The Lorenz Corp.

This little light of mine
African-American spiritual
Public domain

Ubi Caritas
Refrain: from Holy Thursday liturgy
Verses: from 1 Corinthians 13:2-8, by the Taizé Community
Music: Jacques Berthier
© 1979 Les Presses de Taizé (GIA Publications, Inc., agent)

We Are Called
Words (based on Micah 6:8) and music: David Hass
© 1988 GIA Publications

We come to tell our story
See Song of the Body of Christ

We Come to Your Feast
Words and music: Michael Joncas
© 1994 GIA Publications

We Have Been Told
Words and music: David Hass
© 1983 GIA Publications

We Shall Draw Water
Words (based on Isaiah 12:2-6) and
music: Paul Inwood
© 1986 Paul Inwood, published by
OCP Publications

We Shall Rise Again
Words (based on Matthew 11:29-30,
Psalm 23, John 11, 2 Timothy 2) and
music: Jeremy Young
© 1987 GIA Publications, Inc.

We Thank You, Father
Words and music: Gregory Norbet
© The Benedictine Foundation of
the State of Vermont, Inc.

We Three Kings
Words (based on Matthew 2:1-11)
and music: by John H. Hopkins, Jr.
(1820-1891)
Public domain

We Walk by Faith
Words: Henry Alford (1810-1871)
Music: Marty Haugen
Music: © 1984 GIA Publications Inc.

We Were Strangers
Words (based on Ephesians 2:12-16,
Galatians 3:28) and music:
Lucien Deiss
© 1982 Lucien Deiss, published by
OCP Publications

Whatsoever You Do
Words (based on Matthew 5:3-12)
and music: Willard F. Jabusch
© 1966, 1982 Willard F. Jabusch,
published by OCP Publications

Where Charity and Love Prevail
Words: *Ubi Caritas*, translated by
Omer Westendorf (1916-1998)
Music: Paul Benoit, OSB (1893-1979)
© 1961, 1962 World Library
Publications, Inc

Will You Let Me Be Your Servant
Words and music; Richard Gillard
© 1977 Scripture in Song (a division
of Integrity Music)

Ye Sons and Daughters
Words: *O filii et filiae*, attributed to
Jean Tisserand (d. 1494), translated
by John M. Neale (1818-1866)
Public domain

You Are All We Have
Francis Patrick O'Brien
© 1992 GIA Publications, Inc.

You Are Near
Words (based on Psalm 139) and
music: Daniel L. Schutte
© 1971 Daniel L. Schutte, published
by OCP Publications

You Are Mine
Words and music: David Haas
© 1991 GIA Publications, Inc.

Most of the songs suggested for the Sessions can be found in the standard hymnals or parish worship aids. Should you want to get in touch with any of the publishers of the songs suggested (for example, to obtain recorded versions of the songs on CD or cassette, or printed copies of the music scores, or to purchase downloadable PDF, TIFF or MP3 files, or to ask for permission to reprint copyright words), here are their contact details.

The Benedictine Foundation of the State of Vermont, Inc.

58 Priory Hill Road
Weston, VT 05161-6400
Phone   802-824-5409
Fax   802-824-3573
Website   www.westonpriory.org
E-mail   brothers@westonpriory.org

Permissions processed through www.LicenSingonline.org

GIA Publications, Inc.

7404 South Mason Avenue
Chicago, IL 60638
Phone   800-442-1358 or 708-496-3800
Fax   708-496-3828
Website   www.giamusic.com
E-mail   custserv@giamusic.com

For downloadable copies (as PDF or TIFF files, with preview and listen options): www.hymnprint.net

Hope Publishing Company

380 South Main Place
Carol Stream, IL 60188
Phone   800-323-1049 or 630-665-3200
Fax   630-665-2552
Website   www.hopepublishing.com
E-mail   hope@hopepublishing.com

Permissions processed through www.LicenSingonline.org

The Lorenz Corporation

PO Box 802
Dayton, OH 45401
Phone   800-444-1144 or 937-228-6118
Fax   937-223-2042
Website   www.lorenz.com
E-mail   info@lorenz.com

Permissions processed through www.LicenSingonline.org

Oregon Catholic Press Publications (OCP)
5536 NE Hassalo
Portland, OR 97213
Phone   800-LITURGY (548-8749)
Fax   800-4-OCP-FAX (462-7329)
Website   www.ocp.org
E-mail   liturgy@ocp.org

Permissions processed through www.LicenSingonline.org

For downloadable copies in PDF and GIF format:
www.printandpraise.com

Scripture in Song
Maranatha Music
administered by Music Services
1526 Otter Creek Road,
Nashville, TN 37215
Phone   615-371-1320
Fax   615-371-1351
Website   www.musicservices.org
E-mail   info@musicservices.org

spiritandsong.com
PO Box 18030
Portland, OR 97218-0030
Phone   1-800-548-8749
Fax   1-800-462-7329
Website   www.spiritandsong.com
E-mail   support@spiritandsong.com

Permissions processed through www.LicenSingonline.org

Stainer & Bell Ltd
PO Box 110, Victoria House
23 Gruneisen Road
London N3 1DZ
England
Phone   +44 (0)20 8343 3303
Fax   +44 (0)20 8343 3024
Website   www.stainer.co.uk
E-mail   post@stainer.co.uk

Permissions processed through www.LicenSingonline.org

Troubadour for the Lord

Brothers & Sisters of Charity at
Little Portion Hermitage
350 CR 248
Berryville, AR 72631
Phone   877-504-9865 or 479-253-0256
Website   www.troubadourforthelord.com
E-mail   Info@LittlePortion.org

World Library Publications

J. S. Paluch Company, Inc.
3708 River Road, Suite 400
Franklin Park, IL 60131
Phone   800-566-6150
Fax   888-957-3291
Website   www.wlpmusic.com
E-mail   wlpcs@jspaluch.com

Liturgical Calendar

Year C	2012-13	2015-16	2018-19
1st Sunday of Advent	December 2	November 29	December 2
2nd Sunday of Advent	December 9	December 6	December 9
3rd Sunday of Advent	December 16	December 13	December 16
4th Sunday of Advent	December 23	December 20	December 23
The Nativity of the Lord	December 25	December 25	December 25
Holy Family	December 30	December 27	December 30
Mary, Mother of God	January 1	January 1	January 1
Epiphany	January 6	January 3	January 6
Baptism of the Lord	January 13	January 10	January 13
2nd Sunday in Ordinary Time	January 20	January 17	January 20
3rd Sunday in Ordinary Time	January 27	January 24	January 27
Presentation of the Lord	February 2	February 2	February 2
4th Sunday in Ordinary Time	February 3	January 31	February 3
5th Sunday in Ordinary Time	February 10	February 7	February 10
6th Sunday in Ordinary Time	- - -	- - -	February 17
7th Sunday in Ordinary Time	- - -	- - -	February 24
8th Sunday in Ordinary Time	- - -	- - -	March 3
9th Sunday in Ordinary Time	- - -	- - -	- - -
1st Sunday of Lent	February 17	February 14	March 10
2nd Sunday of Lent	February 24	February 21	March 17
3rd Sunday of Lent	March 3	February 28	March 24
4th Sunday of Lent	March 10	March 6	March 31
5th Sunday of Lent	March 17	March 13	April 7
Palm/Passion Sunday	March 24	March 20	April 14
Easter Sunday	March 31	March 27	April 21
2nd Sunday of Easter	April 7	April 3	April 28
3rd Sunday of Easter	April 14	April 10	May 5
4th Sunday of Easter	April 21	April 17	May 12
5th Sunday of Easter	April 28	April 24	May 19
6th Sunday of Easter	May 5	May 1	May 26

Year C	2013	2016	2018
Ascension*	May 9	May 5	June 2
7th Sunday of Easter	May 12	May 8	June 2
Pentecost	May 19	May 15	June 9
Trinity Sunday	May 26	May 22	June 16
The Body and Blood of Christ	June 2	May 29	June 23
9th Sunday in Ordinary Time	---	---	---
10th Sunday in Ordinary Time	June 9	June 5	---
11th Sunday in Ordinary Time	June 16	June 12	---
Nativity of John the Baptist	June 24	June 24	June 24
12th Sunday in Ordinary Time	June 23	June 19	---
St. Peter and St. Paul, Apostles	June 29	June 29	June 29
13th Sunday in Ordinary Time	June 30	June 26	June 30
14th Sunday in Ordinary Time	July 7	July 3	July 7
15th Sunday in Ordinary Time	July 14	July 10	July 14
16th Sunday in Ordinary Time	July 21	July 17	July 21
17th Sunday in Ordinary Time	July 28	July 24	July 28
18th Sunday in Ordinary Time	August 4	July 31	August 4
Transfiguration of the Lord	August 6	August 6	August 6
19th Sunday in Ordinary Time	August 11	August 7	August 11
Assumption	August 15	August 15	August 15
20th Sunday in Ordinary Time	August 18	August 14	August 18
21st Sunday in Ordinary Time	August 25	August 21	August 25
22nd Sunday in Ordinary Time	September 1	August 28	September 1
23rd Sunday in Ordinary Time	September 8	September 4	September 8
The Triumph of the Cross	September 14	September 14	September 14
24th Sunday in Ordinary Time	September 15	September 11	September 15
25th Sunday in Ordinary Time	September 22	September 18	September 22
26th Sunday in Ordinary Time	September 29	September 25	September 29
27th Sunday in Ordinary Time	October 6	October 2	October 6
28th Sunday in Ordinary Time	October 13	October 9	October 13

*   In many places, the Solemnity of the Ascension of the Lord is celebrated on and super-sedes the Seventh Sunday of Easter.

Year C	2013	2016	2018
29th Sunday in Ordinary Time	October 20	October 16	October 20
30th Sunday in Ordinary Time	October 27	October 23	October 27
Solemnity of All Saints	November 1	November 1	November 1
The Commemoration of All Faithfully Departed	November 2	November 2	November 2
31st Sunday in Ordinary Time	November 3	October 30	November 3
The Dedication of the Lateran Basilica	November 9	November 9	November 9
32nd Sunday in Ordinary Time	November 10	November 6	November 10
33rd Sunday in Ordinary Time	November 17	November 13	November 17
34th Sunday/Christ the King	November 24	November 20	November 24

FAITH-SHARING RESOURCES FROM RENEW INTERNATIONAL

Go deeper into the liturgical season with...

Lenten Longings, Years A, B, & C

Lent invites us to a time of prayer, reflection, and conversion. Make a six-week retreat by exploring the Sunday readings of Lent. Simple language and everyday metaphors steep you in the season's promptings to surrender self, work for justice, and deepen prayer life. *Lenten Longings* is well suited for seasonal groups, small Christian communities, and individual reflection.

Let Yourself Be ... —Year A
For the Life of the World—Year B
Seeing with God's Eyes—Year C

Also available as an eBook!

 This 18-song CD contains the songs suggested for use during the prayerful reflections of each faith-sharing session for years A, B, and C.

Disponible en español: **Reflexiones en Cuaresma, Años A, B, y C**

Advent Awakenings, Years A, B, & C

Advent is a time of spiritual anticipation amidst the often distracting preparations for Christmas. Stay focused on the significance of this season with *Advent Awakenings*. Each book contains four sessions corresponding with the four Sundays of Advent and presents themes drawn from the Sunday gospel readings, plus enriching devotions for family use.

Trust the Lord—Year A
Take the Time—Year B
Say Yes to God—Year C

Also available as an eBook!

 This 15-song CD contains the songs suggested for use during the prayerful reflections of each faith-sharing session for years A, B, and C.

Disponible en español: **Reflexiones en Adviento, Años A, B, y C**

At Prayer with Mary

At Prayer with Mary offers seven sessions on the life and mystery of Mary that will deepen your appreciation of and devotion to our Blessed Mother Mary and enrich your prayer experiences. Mary, the mother of Jesus, has been revered since the earliest days of the Church. Over the centuries, her example has inspired Christians to imitate her by saying "yes" to God's call in their own lives. Mary's faithfulness, as it is portrayed in the Gospel narratives, is a model of the prayerful kind of life Jesus calls us to. Scripture, Catholic teaching, personal 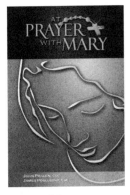 testimonies, and Marian prayer—including the rosary—provide a renewed appreciation of Mary's place in today's world, where she, as always, points the way to Christ.

Also available as an eBook!

 CD is also available and contains the songs suggested for use during the moments of prayer.

Disponible en español: **No temas, María**

Scenes from a Parish
Special Edition DVD
and Film Faith Sharing Guides
In English and Spanish

Get a rare glimpse into one parish's real-world experience as it struggles to reconcile ideals of faith with the realities of today's changing and diverse culture. View, reflect upon, and share faith with this special edition film and *Faith-Sharing Guide* and its important themes of welcoming the stranger, offering compassion, and feeding the hungry.

Ideal for parish-wide, small group, and personal viewing and reflection.

LONGING FOR THE HOLY: Spirituality for Everyday Life
Based on selected insights of Ronald Rolheiser, O.M.I.

Experience how the gentle spiritual guidance and practical wisdom of best-selling Catholic author Fr. Ronald Rolheiser, O.M.I. can enliven everyday life. Suitable for small community faith sharing or individual reflection, *Longing for the Holy* covers different dimensions of contemporary spiritual life for those who want to enrich their sense of the presence of God and develop a deeper spirituality.

The Participant's Book contains twelve sessions with prayers, reflections, sharing questions, and stories from saints and contemporary people of faith.

This resource is also available as a four CD-set audio edition, which has both narrated text and songs for all twelve sessions.

The songs suggested for the moments of prayer in the faith-sharing sessions are offered on this 13-song anthology CD.

Disponible en español: ***Sedientos de Dios: una espiritualidad para la gente de hoy***